my cousin rosa

rosa mitchell's sicilian kitchen

MURDOCH BOOKS

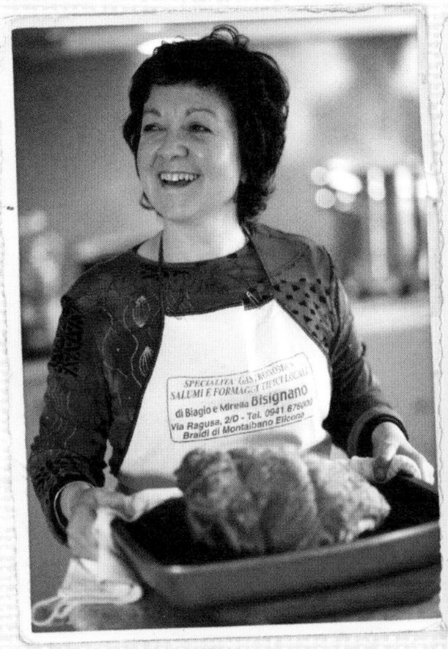

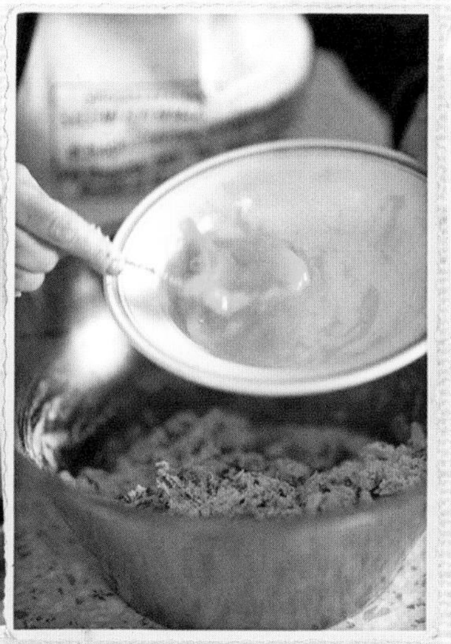

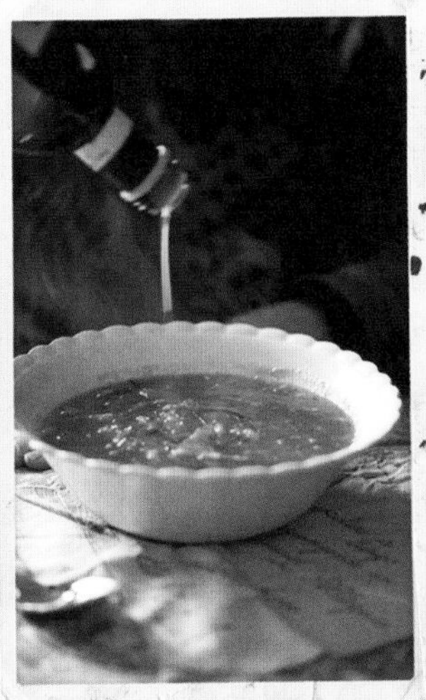

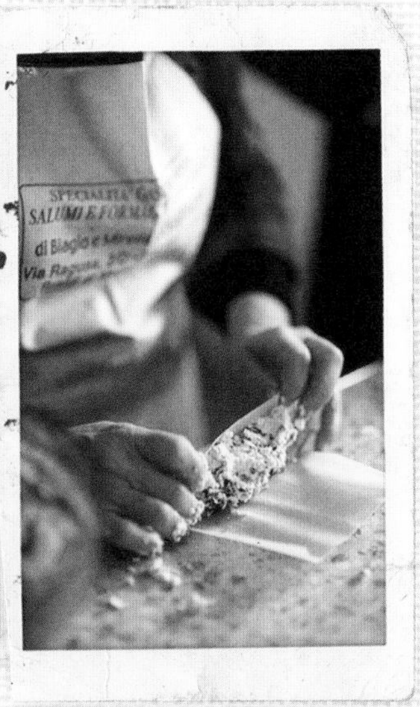

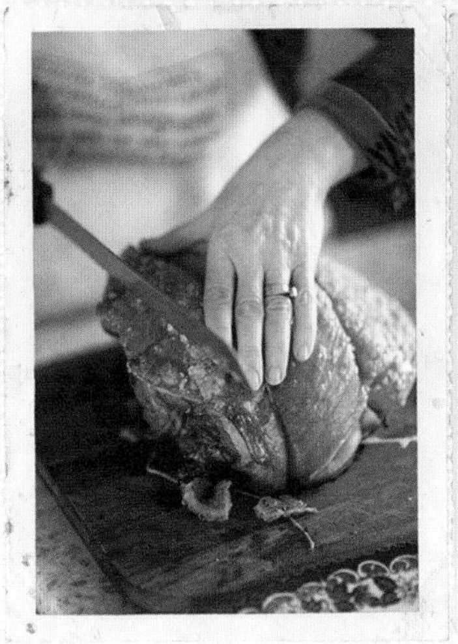

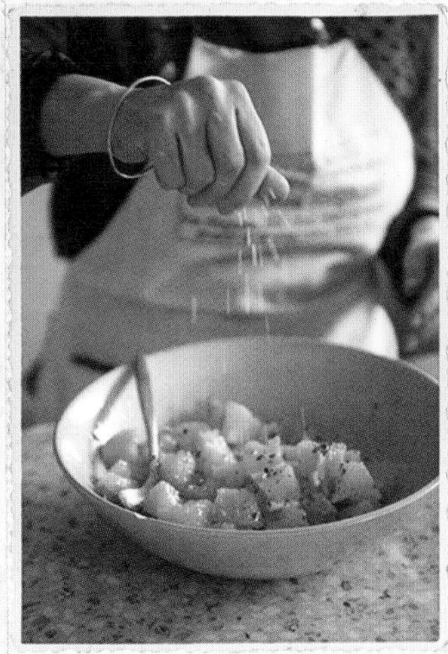

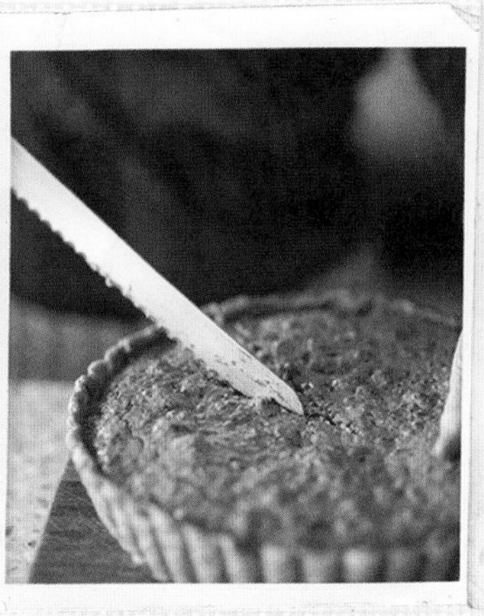

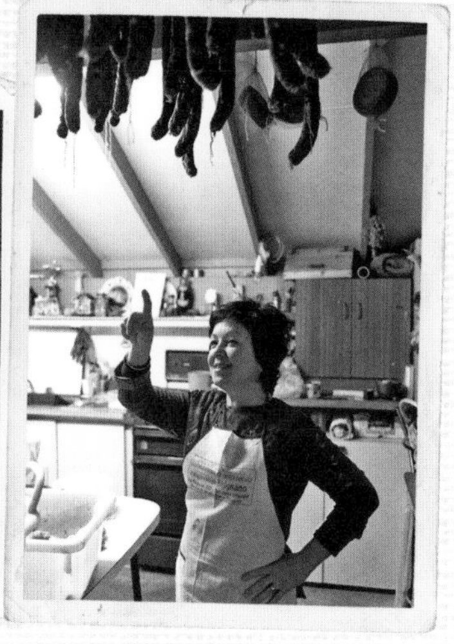

a sicilian kitchen in australia

Both my parents came from the same region of Messina, way up in the Sicilian mountains, just a few villages apart. I was born in the city of Catania, my parents having moved there after they were married when my father was searching for a job. This was very different to life in the mountain villages of their parents, which was very poor and they grew their own vegetables and made cheese, salami and preserves to keep them going well into the winter months. A lot of the younger people from the villages moved away to look for work; some to the bigger northern Italian cities and others overseas.

Some of my strongest memories of Sicily are of visiting my grandparents. My father's father would take me on his donkey, Mariano, to visit my mother's family. Along the way he would climb the stone walls and pick grapes for us to eat. It would take us about an hour to go down and up the mountains.

My father worked at an orchard and his brother lived on the adjoining property, so once a week Papa would take me and my mother to visit on his bicycle. My cousins and I would play under the orange trees while my mother and aunt would bake the week's supply of bread. Then it was off home: my father, my mother and a week's supply of bread all on the bicycle. (For the first few years in Australia my father did everything on his bike, collecting building materials and anything else he could fit on it.)

My grandfather decided that life in Sicily was too hard and held no future. He left his family with much regret (he had 10 children at home and one married) and travelled alone to find a better life in Australia. He knew of a family from his village who were successful in Melbourne, running market gardens, but he didn't know how to find them. The Victorian fruit and vegetable market seemed a good place to start and by sheer luck he ran into the man and was offered work in the market gardens of Werribee South.

Twelve months later two sons followed him, then another, and finally the rest of the family. We arrived two years later: my parents, myself and my little brother Pep (Giuseppe). It was 1962. The trip was long and I remember tasting butter and drinking tea for the first time and I disliked both. My mother was happy to be with her family again; life continued much as it had done in Sicily, with get-togethers to make macaroni, salami, tomato sugo and preserves. In those days we would all make our traditional foods together. Now our family numbers over 130 and a lot of preserving is done in smaller family groups accompanied by much good-natured rivalry ('my salami is better than yours' and such). I am just happy that we're still keeping up the traditions.

I like to make the basic foods my parents and grandparents ate all their lives back home. Making food is not just something we do to survive; it's the coming together and sharing, chatting and arguing over the methods and superstitions. We like to gather wild fennel, cardoons and nettles from the side of the road (although this is getting harder because of urban spread). We pass down recipes for biscuits and enjoy arguing over when to salt our vegetables. One thing that concerns me is that in Italy and Australia, people are starting to lose their traditions. In years to come, who is going to make the salami or sugo or the preserves, or even just the simple traditional meals? We are all so busy that it seems easier to open a tin or have take-away, when really some meals are quicker to prepare than we think. Good produce, cooked simply and enjoyed with family and friends is what it's all about.

antipasto

Sicilians love not only their food but also the opportunity to come together for animated conversation while mama is cooking the meal. Antipasto nibbles stimulate the appetite and the conversation. Antipasto for us is an everyday treat — it might be as simple as slices of salami or cheese with olives or a little fritter.

insalata di olive
marinated olives

I like to pit the olives myself — I find commercially pitted olives are often too soft and the unpitted ones have a better flavour. It is easy enough to pit them: just use a flat-bottomed bottle or meat tenderiser, give them a little bang and remove the stone.

500 g (1 lb 2 oz/3 cups) firm green olives in brine
3 celery stalks from the heart of the celery, thinly sliced
1 small carrot, thinly sliced
2 garlic cloves, crushed
1 tablespoon dried oregano
1 teaspoon aniseeds
1 teaspoon chilli flakes (optional)
125 ml (4 fl oz/½ cup) extra virgin olive oil
3 tablespoons white wine vinegar

Mix all the ingredients together and leave them to marinate for 2–3 hours before serving so that the flavours have time to meld. These can be stored in the fridge for up to 4 days but let them come back to room temperature before serving.
(Serves 8–10)

carciofi sott' olio
preserved artichokes

This might seem like a lot of artichokes but by the time you've cleaned one it will look much smaller! Feel free to use more artichokes if you like, but the vinegar and water cooking liquid can stay the same. I like to use the purple and green artichoke varieties as they have less choke in the centre. When preserving artichokes it's best to wait until later in the season when they are cheaper and, if you are lucky, you'll be able to buy the smaller ones. I haven't specified how much oil you'll need here because it will depend on what size jars you use. If you buy a 4-litre tin (and you don't need expensive stuff), it should be more than enough.

6 kg (13–14 lb) globe artichokes
4 lemons
3 litres (12 cups) white wine vinegar
125 g (4½ oz/1 cup) salt
6 fresh bay leaves

6 garlic cloves, peeled and cut in half
1 tablespoon fennel seeds
1 tablespoon chilli flakes (optional)
olive oil

Clean the artichokes by snapping off the tough outer leaves until you start to see leaves with a tender yellowy base. Trim the stalk by peeling gently around the base, where you have pulled off the leaves. Leave the stalk about 2–3 cm (1 inch) long. Cut in half and remove the furry choke if there is one. Put in a plastic bucket full of water into which you've squeezed the juice of the lemons (throw in the lemons as well, for good luck). This will prevent the artichokes discolouring.

Put the vinegar and salt in a large pot (not aluminium) and add 3 litres (12 cups) water. Bring to the boil and add some artichokes (you will probably need to cook them in 3 or 4 batches). Boil gently for about 15–25 minutes, depending on the size of the artichokes. Have a taste; they should be al dente. If they are too soft they will eventually become mushy in the jar.

Using tongs, remove the artichokes from the boiling liquid, drain and place, cut side down, on a tray lined with a tea towel. Let them cool completely and then half-fill a sterilised jar with artichokes. Place 1–2 bay leaves, a couple of garlic cloves, a sprinkle of fennel seeds and a sprinkle of chilli (if you're using it) into the jar. Fill with more artichokes, pressing down a little so there are no gaps, and another layer of herbs and spices.

Fill the jar with olive oil and leave for an hour, then top up with more oil if needed and seal. The artichokes will keep for up to 1 year under the oil, but if exposed they will go mouldy. (Makes enough to fill 1 medium-sized jar)

pomodori sott' olio
sun-dried tomatoes

True sun-dried tomatoes are a taste sensation. A lot of the commercial varieties you find today are not sun-dried at all, so they lack that wonderful concentration of flavour. Have a go during the summer and you will not be disappointed. If you grow your own tomatoes this is a great way to preserve them. There is no point in my giving you quantities here as they will completely depend on the amount of tomatoes you are drying. This is a simple recipe but time-consuming (in a relaxing sort of way).

> **tomatoes**
> **salt**
> **garlic cloves, peeled and cut in half**
> **dried oregano**
> **basil leaves**
> **fennel seeds**
> **olive oil**

Cut your tomatoes in half, place cut side up on a wire rack and sprinkle liberally with salt. Put them outside in the sun. It will depend how hot the sun is as to how long they will need. The tomatoes will start to lose their moisture, and they must be brought inside every night and not get wet. They need to be quite dry but not hard or they will become leathery.

When you think your tomatoes are ready, bring them in and rinse them quickly with hot water to remove any dust or salt that remains. Dry them quickly and place on a wire rack in a 120°C (235°F/Gas ½) oven for about 15 minutes or until they dry again. Leave to cool completely, and then start to layer into a sterilised jar. Add a few pieces of garlic, a sprinkle of oregano, a couple of basil leaves and some fennel seeds to each jar and then another layer of tomatoes. Repeat until the jar is full.

Fill the jars with olive oil and leave for 30 minutes to settle. The oil level will drop as it seeps in between the tomatoes, so top up the oil and seal. The tomatoes need to sit for 1 month before they are ready to be eaten. They will last in the jar, under oil, for up to 2 years.
(Makes however many tomatoes you started with...)

melanzane sott' olio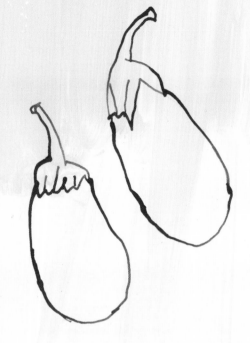
preserved eggplant

3 kg (7 lb) eggplants (aubergines), firm and fresh
125 g (4½ oz/1 cup) salt
2 litres (8 cups) vinegar
6 garlic cloves, peeled and cut in half
1 tablespoon fennel seeds
1 tablespoon dried oregano
chilli flakes (optional)
1–2 litres (4–8 cups) olive oil

Peel the eggplants (I know, but it is worth it), then cut widthways into slices about 1 cm (½ inch) thick. Then cut each slice into 1 cm (½ inch) strips. Spread out evenly in a large deep tray, and sprinkle with the salt. Leave for 24 hours, uncovered and at room temperature.

You'll find the eggplant will have produced a lot of liquid, so stir the eggplant in this liquid and then drain well. I put the slices in a colander and put a weight on top to extract as much liquid as possible. Rinse and dry the tray and place the eggplant back in the tray. Pour on the vinegar, stir and push the eggplant under the vinegar. Leave for 24 hours, uncovered and at room temperature. Drain in a colander, putting a weight on the eggplant to drain off as much liquid as possible. Leave draining for about 4 hours.

Put the eggplant in a large bowl with the garlic, fennel seeds, oregano, chilli (if using) and 250 ml (9 fl oz/1 cup) olive oil and mix well. Transfer to sterilised jars, push down with a wooden spoon, then top up with olive oil and seal. The eggplant should be ready to eat in about 1 month, or can be kept for about 1 year.
(Makes enough to fill 1 large or 2 medium-sized jars)

bianchetti fritti
fried whitebait

500 g (1 lb 2 oz) whitebait (they should be about 3–4 cm/1–2 inches long)
150 g (5 oz/1 cup) plain (all-purpose) flour, for dusting
1 litre (35 fl oz/4 cups) vegetable oil, for frying
fine sea salt
lemon wedges

Sort through the whitebait and take out any that are damaged. I like to rinse them in cold running water and then pat them dry.

Put the flour in a flat bowl and season with salt and pepper. Heat the oil in a large saucepan to 190°C (375°F) — if you drop one fish into the oil and it sizzles, the oil is ready for cooking. Toss the whitebait in the flour a few at a time, shake off the excess and lower them into the oil.

Cook for about 2 minutes or until golden. Drain on kitchen paper and sprinkle with the sea salt. Serve with lemon wedges.

(Serves 6)

fritelli di cavolfiore
cauliflower fritters

½ large cauliflower
300 g (10 oz/2 cups) self-raising flour
100 g (3½ oz/1 cup) grated parmesan cheese
1 garlic clove, crushed
3 tablespoons chopped Italian (flat-leaf) parsley
3 eggs, lightly beaten
olive oil, for frying

Break up all the cauliflower into small pieces. Bring a pot of salted water to the boil, add the cauliflower and cook until soft (push a fork through a bit of stalk and if it goes through easily the cauliflower is cooked). Drain and cool in a bowl.

Add the flour, cheese, garlic, parsley and some salt and pepper to the cauliflower and mix lightly. Add the beaten eggs and mix again. If the mixture is too dry, add a little water to just bring it together.

Heat enough oil to cover the base of a frying pan over medium heat. When hot, add tablespoons of the mixture, taking care not to overcrowd them. Cook until golden, turn over and flatten slightly with a fork. Cook on the other side until golden and cooked through to the centre. Serve hot or at room temperature as a pre-dinner snack.
(Makes about 20)

fritelle di cardone
cardoon fritters

Cardoons are actually Scottish thistles (yes, Scottish thistles) that grow wild on the outskirts of Melbourne. (Also, some Italian delis here do sell the seeds.) In Sicily everyone is out looking for them, but here they are seen as weeds. The right time to pick them is June–August when the plant is young. Once it has started to flower, the cardoon is too tough. Look for a healthy upright plant and, using a sharp knife, cut it at the base (be careful: it has prickles, so gloves are a good idea). We are only using the stems here so, with your knife, run along the edges and take off the leaves. The stems should be tender, so if they are at all fibrous discard them.

Cardoons have a slight bitterness to them but, once cooked, they are delicious. They are favoured by a lot of Europeans (and are grown commercially on some parts of the continent — the cultivated variety don't have the prickles so they are easier to handle). If you can't find cardoons you could use artichoke stems here.

1 kg (2 lb 4 oz) cardoon stems, cut into 8 cm (3 inch) pieces, then halved lengthways
225 g (8 oz/1½ cups) self-raising flour
100 g (3½ oz/1 cup) grated parmesan cheese
1 garlic clove, crushed
2 tablespoons chopped Italian (flat-leaf) parsley
3 eggs, lightly beaten
olive oil, for frying

Bring a pot of salted water to the boil, add the cardoons and cook until soft. It is hard to say how long to cook them for as it will depend on their tenderness, but keep checking. You want to be able to push a fork through them easily. I have found it can take anything from 10 minutes to 45 minutes. Drain and cool in a bowl. Add the flour, cheese, garlic, parsley and some salt and pepper and mix lightly. Add the beaten eggs and mix again. If it seems too dry, add a little water to bring it together.

Heat enough oil to cover the base of a frying pan over medium heat. When hot, add tablespoons of the mixture and cook for about 4 minutes until golden. Turn over and flatten slightly with a fork. Cook on the other side until golden and cooked through to the centre. Serve hot or at room temperature.

(Makes 15–20)

I love collecting food in the wild. My mother and I will search for cardoons along the side of railway lines, armed with a basket and a couple of sharp knives. (Driving along country roads I am always screeching to a halt to collect wild fennel seeds, rabe, rocket, stinging nettles or blackberries.)

olive siciliane
sicilian-style pickled olives

Buy your fresh olives from the market or good fruit shops. They should be green with no tinge of black. The season is very short so be on the lookout for them. If you have your own tree, which seems to be quite popular these days, they should be picked when they turn from bright green to yellow green and seem to plump up a little more than usual.

I haven't specified the amount of oil you'll need because it will depend entirely on how many jars you use and the size of your olives. A 4-litre tin should be ample.

2 kg (4½ lb) fresh green olives	3 tablespoons dried oregano
6 lemons	2 tablespoons dried aniseeds
450 g (1 lb/1½ cups) coarse salt	fresh bay leaves (optional)
1 litre (35 fl oz/4 cups) white vinegar	1 tablespoon chilli flakes (optional)
5 garlic cloves, peeled and cut in half	olive oil

Pit your olives: using a flat-bottomed bottle or meat tenderiser, give each one a little bang; it should crack open and you can remove the stone (wear gloves as the olives stain your hands). Do a few at a time, then put them in a large bowl of cold water into which you've sliced 3 of the lemons. When you've pitted all the olives give them a stir in the water, then drain them. Fill the bowl again with cold water (the ratio should be about one part olives to three parts water), add the other lemons, sliced, and about ½ cup of the salt. Leave the olives in this water for 24 hours.

Drain the olives well and transfer them to a deep tray that will hold them all. Loosely sprinkle with the rest of the salt and again leave for 24 hours. The salt will turn to liquid so mix the olives in this liquid, then drain very well. Rinse the tray, put the drained olives back in the tray, pour the vinegar over the olives and leave again for 24 hours.

Drain the olives, return to the tray and add the garlic, oregano, aniseeds, bay leaves and chilli flakes (if using). Mix well together. Now you can use small sterilised jars or 2 or 3 larger jars. (I like to use smaller jars because I give them as gifts.) Divide the olives evenly among the jars, trying to get a few pieces of garlic into each jar. Top up each jar with olive oil until all the olives are covered. Let them sit for about an hour for the oil to settle. If you need to top up the oil again, do so; if not, place a bay leaf on top of each jar, seal and leave for about 2–3 weeks before eating. These will keep for about 12 months.

olive fritte
fried black olives

4 tablespoons olive oil

375 g (13 oz/2 cups) preserved firm black olives

1 teaspoon chilli flakes

2 garlic cloves, peeled and cut in half

1 rosemary sprig

Heat the oil in a frying pan, add the olives, chilli flakes, garlic and rosemary. Cook the olives, tossing constantly, for about 10 minutes or until soft to touch. Place in a bowl and serve warm. This makes a great pre-dinner snack.

(Serves 4)

peperoni arrostiti
grilled peppers

10–12 long red capsicums (peppers)

3 tablespoons extra virgin olive oil

a handful of basil leaves

4 anchovies or 2 tablespoons capers

Heat your oven to its highest temperature. Put the capsicums on a baking tray in the oven and cook, turning once or twice, for about 30–40 minutes, or until the skins start turning black. Put them in a bowl, cover with plastic wrap and leave to cool. When cool, peel away the skins. I never rinse them under water as this removes the beautiful natural juices.

Rip the capsicums apart or chop them roughly. Place in a bowl with the oil, basil leaves and anchovies or capers (not both, or they will be overpowering) and salt. Mix gently before serving.

(Serves 6)

favi fritti
fried broad beans

500 g (1 lb 2 oz) dried broad beans
250 ml (9 fl oz/1 cup) vegetable oil
sea salt
chilli powder or paprika

Soak the broad beans in plenty of water for 2 days, changing the water once. Drain and peel the beans. (The peeling is time-consuming, but with some help it shouldn't take too long.) After removing the outer skin, pull the bean apart gently. Arrange the beans on a dry tea towel and place another tea towel over them. I leave them overnight to dry as much as possible.

Half-fill a small but deep saucepan with oil — only fill it halfway because when you add the beans it will boil rapidly. Heat the oil to 180°C (350°F) or until a bean dropped into the oil bubbles. Be careful when you cook these as the oil is very hot — only add about ½ cupful of beans to the pan at a time, no more. Cook for about 5 minutes, giving them a little stir so that they are evenly spaced in the pan. They should turn golden (if they brown too quickly turn the heat down). Drain on kitchen paper and, when cool enough to handle but still warm, place in a bowl and sprinkle with the salt and chilli or paprika and toss well. These will keep in an airtight container for 2–3 months.

insalata di orzo
barley salad

This is lovely as part of an antipasto plate or as a side dish with a main meal. In Sicily this salad is usually made with wheatberries but they can prove difficult to find. If you do find them, they need to be soaked for at least 24 hours, then boiled for about 3 hours. Then mixed with the other ingredients.

250 g (9 oz) barley
1 garlic clove, crushed
3 large ripe tomatoes, finely chopped
½ red onion, very finely chopped
3 tablespoons chopped mint
125 ml (4 fl oz/½ cup) extra virgin olive oil
3 tablespoons red wine vinegar or lemon juice

Soak the barley overnight, then drain well in a colander. Boil the barley in plenty of water for 20–30 minutes until tender. Drain and rinse with cold water. Let the barley cool completely before using.

Mix the barley, garlic, tomatoes, onion and mint together. Whisk together the oil and vinegar and season with salt and pepper, then pour over the salad and toss. Serve at room temperature. (Serves 6)

🌺 ricotta fritta
fried ricotta

**When I cook with ricotta I always like to buy it in a large round from the deli —
I find it is a firmer variety than the cheese you get in the smaller tubs. If you can
only buy the tubs, drain the ricotta overnight in a colander over a bowl to remove
as much liquid as possible.**

300 g (10 oz) fresh firm ricotta
4 tablespoons olive oil
2 eggs, lightly beaten

Cut the ricotta into small flat pieces. Heat the oil in a non-stick frying pan over medium heat. Dip
the ricotta into the beaten eggs and then place in the frying pan. Keep going until the bottom of
the frying pan is covered but not overcrowded.

Sprinkle the ricotta pieces with a little salt and cook for about 2 minutes until golden. Flip the
pieces over, salt again and cook the other side until golden. Drain on a plate lined with kitchen
paper while you cook the rest. Serve warm or at room temperature as part of an antipasto platter,
as a side dish or even in a sandwich.

(Serves 6)

frittata

Frittata in my childhood home was often leftover vegies combined with egg to make a meal. In a Sicilian household nothing is wasted, so any leftovers such as asparagus, zucchini, fennel, radicchio, peas, even onions, are used. If you're using larger pieces of vegetable, chop them fairly finely to make your frittata easier to slice. The frittata is very thin; the egg is just there to bring the vegetables together. This is a basic recipe so feel free to use any vegetables you wish — some great combinations are pea and prosciutto or zucchini and parmesan shavings. Frittata makes a wonderful sandwich filling for school lunches.

4 tablespoons olive oil
2 cupfuls chopped cooked vegetables
4 eggs, lightly beaten
2 tablespoons grated parmesan cheese

Heat the oil in a non-stick 20 cm (8 inch) frying pan. When it's hot, add your vegetables and season if necessary. Spread the vegetables evenly over the bottom of the pan. Beat the eggs with the parmesan, pour evenly over the vegetables and turn the heat to medium. Make sure that the egg is evenly spread, and cook for about 5 minutes. I will often lift the edges of the frittata and let the egg run in underneath.

There are two ways to finish off: one is to place the frittata in a hot oven for about 5 minutes until the egg has cooked on top; or you can put a dinner plate on top of the frittata in the pan and then flip the frittata out and then slide it off the plate back into the frying pan. I find the frittata doesn't dry out as much this way, but it can be tricky to do at first. It tastes good either way. (Serves 2–4)

pasta per pizza o pane
pizza or bread dough

30 g (1 oz) fresh yeast or 2 x 7 g (¼ oz) sachets dried yeast
2 teaspoons sugar
700 g (1 lb 9 oz) unbleached plain (all-purpose) flour, or Italian pizza flour
2–3 teaspoons salt
5 tablespoons olive oil

Crumble the fresh yeast into 185 ml (6 fl oz/¾ cup) of water and add the sugar. Stir until the yeast dissolves. (If you're using dried yeast, mix the water with the sugar, then sprinkle the yeast over the top.) Leave in a warm place for 10–15 minutes, until the yeast starts to become frothy.

Sift the flour and salt into a large bowl and make a well in the centre. Pour in the yeast mixture, the oil and another 185 ml (6 fl oz/¾ cup) of water. Mix well with your hands: if it's too dry add a little more warm water, or if too wet add a little more flour. Knead the dough until soft and elastic, sprinkling with a little flour if it's a bit too sticky. I usually knead the dough in the bowl, but you can do it on a floured surface if you like and then tip it back into the bowl.

Roll the dough into a ball, wet a tea towel, fold in half and place over the bowl. Leave in a warm place for about 1½ hours, until it has doubled in size and is ready to use.
(Makes enough for 2 pizza bases)

schiaciatta
broccoli pie

This is a traditional Sicilian broccoli pie. Some families arrange slices of raw potato over the dough before placing the broccoli on top.

3 heads of broccoli
6 spring onions (scallions), thinly sliced
100 g (3½ oz/1 cup) grated parmesan cheese
125 ml (4 fl oz/½ cup) olive oil, plus 3 tablespoons extra
6 anchovy fillets (optional)
½ teaspoon chilli flakes (optional)
1 quantity pizza dough (page 38)

Preheat the oven to 190°C (375°F/Gas 5). You need a baking dish that measures about 30 x 35 cm (12 x 14 inches). Cut the broccoli into thin pieces, taking off some of the stalk from the bottom but not too much. Wash and drain the broccoli and put in a large bowl with the spring onions, parmesan, ½ cup of olive oil, anchovies and chilli flakes (if using) and some salt and pepper. Mix well with your hands.

Halve the pizza dough and roll out one piece to about the same size as your dish. Use some of the extra olive oil to brush the bottom of the dish and then line the dish with the dough, using your fingers to stretch it out to cover the whole bottom of the dish. Gently place all the broccoli on top of the dough (it seems like a lot, but the broccoli does reduce down), leaving a gap all the way around the edge.

Roll out the second piece of dough and place on top of the broccoli. Seal the edges all around by pinching the dough. It needs to be sealed properly as the steam trapped inside will cook the broccoli.

Brush the top with olive oil and bake for 1–1¼ hours until a lovely light golden. Take out of the oven and leave for at least 30 minutes before cutting and serving. This dish is as good cold as it is warm.

(Serves 12, or 6 as a meal)

pane fritto
fried bread

You can make this fried bread any shape or size you like; I usually make them about 3 cm wide and 12 cm long, but it really doesn't matter.

½ quantity bread dough (page 38)
anchovies (optional)
olive oil, for frying
good-quality sea salt

Cut the dough into small pieces and then flatten them with your fingers (flour your fingers if necessary to prevent sticking). If you're using the anchovies, make the pieces of dough slightly larger, place an anchovy fillet in the centre, fold and seal by pressing the edges with your fingers.

Cover the base of a large non-stick frying pan with oil and heat it up. When the oil is hot, add the dough pieces, not too many at once. After about 2 minutes, when they start to bubble and become slightly brown at the edges, turn them over and cook the other side. If they start to burn, turn the heat down a little.

Sprinkle with salt and serve at once. These can be eaten on their own or as a side for a main meal.

(Serves 6–8)

My mother was devastated when her family emigrated to Australia. This photo was taken in the beautiful park in our Sicilian hometown of Catania. My mother's two brothers, Carmelo and Mario, are on their way to Australia. Two years later we could bear it no longer: we followed and joined the family.

 salami

Sicilians love making salami. This is a two-day event that takes place in Australia during the first full moon of June. Salami needs to be made when the weather is cool so it doesn't spoil while hanging. We make our salami with my parents, brothers, their partners, our children and friends and a good time is had by all.

Traditionally in Sicily, pigs were bred from young for the sole purpose of making salami. Here in Australia we buy our meat from good butchers who specialise in pork for salami. The pigs are usually about 200 kg dressed weight and by the time we've separated the meat from the bones and the skin we are left with about 90–100 kg of salami meat. The meat is then minced and seasoned with salt and spices and mixed by hand for about 15 minutes before being left overnight.

My mother will usually have a huge pot on the heat where she boils up some of the meat bones and skin to make a brawn-like loaf, and then lard.

When my grandmother was alive she would use the leftovers to make a soap — greyish and smelly, but effective (nothing goes to waste).

The next day we fill the casings (the cleaned intestines) with the seasoned meat, tying them ready to hang. The thinner ones are hung for about 4–6 weeks, the larger ones up to 12 weeks, depending on their size and the weather. We hang them in my father's garage and it's quite a sight. We love sharing them with family and friends while at the same time trying to make them last until next year's come along. They never do.

pork and fennel salami

6 kg (13–14 lb) pork, coarsely chopped in a mincer
2 kg (4½ lb) pork fat, finely chopped
240 g (9 oz) salt (usually 30 g/1 oz per 1 kg/2 lb 4 oz of meat)
crushed black pepper, to taste
chilli flakes, to taste
fennel seeds, whole or ground, to taste
sausage casings (from your butcher), soaked in water overnight
4 lemons

I haven't specified exact amounts for the spices because this is such a personal thing. If you like your salami spicy, shake in a lot of chilli flakes. Mix together the meat, pork fat, salt, pepper, chilli flakes and fennel seeds and then leave the mixture to stand for at least 3 hours or overnight.

When all the flavours have blended together, fry a tiny bit of your mixture in a frying pan and taste it to check you're happy with the seasonings. It will taste salty, but the salt is the preservative so you need that amount to keep it from going off.

The sausage casings are the pig's intestines and come in several sizes from skinny to large. You buy them from the butcher, but may need to order them in advance. Wash them very gently in fresh water and lemon juice about three or four times and keep the casings you aren't using in the water while you fill the salami — they need to be wet at all times.

You'll need a special attachment for your mincer for filling the salami. Fill the casings gently and slowly (you don't want any air pockets or the meat will oxidise and go bad). As each casing is filled, tie at the end and prick gently with a sewing needle to release any air.

Once filled, your salami should hang in an airy well-ventilated space such as a garage or cellar for 6 weeks to 3 months, depending on the casings you've used. The salami should feel firm when they're ready. Cryovac them and keep in a cool place (they don't need refrigeration). This recipe also makes wonderful sausages: just cut down the salt by half. Once made, the sausages can be frozen.

At school in Sicily we all wore these navy blue smocks over our clothes. When I arrived in Australia, even though I was seven, I was so tiny that the teachers thought I was younger and I was put in a preschool class. The novice nun drew a large 'A' on a piece of paper and motioned for me to have a go. Everyone was very impressed when I copied it perfectly. I was surprised and rather dismissive of their praise —in Sicily I'd been making up stories in joined-up writing.

brodo

Most of the soups eaten in our house when I was growing up were quite substantial meals: hearty and thick, often with lots of legumes. In the winter months, when not so many fresh vegetables were to be found, lentils, chickpeas and dried beans made a good substitute.

🌺 zuppa di ceci, porri e patate
chickpea, leek and potato soup

Chickpeas are very temperamental. I have found that some of the supermarket varieties are tough and don't seem to cook very well. I always buy my chickpeas from good delis and, even though I have instructed to cook them for an hour, it could vary, so check them as you go. You need them to be cooked until quite soft here. My family have a superstition that you can only stir chickpeas or other legumes with a wooden spoon: they believe that using a metal spoon toughens them. (I'm not at all superstitious, but I only ever use a wooden spoon!)

To salt or not to salt? Some people don't salt legumes until the very end of cooking because they think the salt hardens them. My feeling is that salting them halfway through the cooking gives them time to absorb the salt and makes them tastier than if you salt them at the end.

660 g (1½ lb/3 cups) dried chickpeas
3 tablespoons olive oil
1 large onion, diced
4 leeks, thinly sliced
3 potatoes (spunta are good), peeled and diced
extra virgin olive oil, to serve

Soak the chickpeas overnight in about 3 litres (12 cups) of cold water. Drain the chickpeas and place in a large pot with a fresh 3 litres of cold water and bring to a gentle boil. Turn down the heat and leave to simmer for about 1 hour.

Meanwhile, heat the olive oil in a large frying pan and cook the onion and leeks gently for about 15 minutes until quite soft. Add to the chickpeas along with the potatoes, season with salt and pepper and cook for a further 30 minutes over medium heat. I like to serve this soup with a drizzle of extra virgin olive oil.

(Serves 6)

zuppa di piselli e carciofi
pea and artichoke soup

8 globe artichokes
2 lemons
125 ml (4 fl oz/½ cup) olive oil
2 onions, finely chopped
1 kg (2 lb 4 oz) frozen peas
extra virgin olive oil, to serve

Clean the artichokes by snapping off the tough outer leaves until you start to see leaves with a tender yellowy base. Trim the stalk by peeling gently around the base, where you have pulled off the leaves. Leave the stalk about 2–3 cm (1 inch) long. Cut in half and remove the furry choke if there is one. As you prepare them, put them in a bowl of water with the juice of the lemons (and throw the lemons in as well).

Heat the oil in a saucepan over medium heat and fry the onions until translucent. Drain the artichokes, slice them finely and add to the onions.

I like to rinse the frozen peas in a colander with water before I use them. Add the peas to the pan and stir well. Cook for about 15 minutes, then turn down the heat to low, add 250 ml (9 fl oz/1 cup) of water, cover and cook slowly for about 1 hour. The secret here is to let the vegetables cook in only a little liquid so that they stew in their own juices, but you will need to top up the water if it looks like drying up. After 1 hour, add 2–3 litres (8–12 cups) of hot water and cook for a further 30 minutes. Serve with a drizzle of extra virgin olive oil.
(Serves 6–8)

zuppa con broccoli e patate
broccoli and potato soup

1 kg (2 lb 4 oz) broccoli
125 ml (4 fl oz/½ cup) olive oil
1 large onion, finely chopped
1 garlic clove, finely chopped
2 leeks, thinly sliced
4 potatoes (spunta are good), peeled and diced

Wash the broccoli. Cut off the florets and cut into small pieces. Chop the stalks finely. Heat the oil in a large pot and gently cook the onion, garlic, leeks and broccoli stalks for about 15 minutes, stirring often, until the broccoli stalks are tender. You may need to add ½ cupful of water to prevent the vegetables sticking, but add the water a little at a time as you go along.

Add the broccoli florets and potatoes. Cook for about 10 minutes, then add enough water to cover, season with salt and cook for a further 30 minutes. Don't worry if you overcook this soup a bit — it all adds to the final flavour.

(Serves 6)

minestra di lenticchie e pasta
lentil soup with pasta

4 tablespoons olive oil
1 onion, finely chopped
3 celery stalks, finely chopped
1 carrot, finely chopped
500 g (1 lb 2 oz) lentils
250 g (9 oz) small pasta
2 small heads of broccoli or ½ bunch silverbeet, finely chopped
extra virgin olive oil, to serve

Heat the oil in a large pot over medium heat, add the onion, celery and carrot and cook for about 10 minutes. Meanwhile, wash the lentils in cold water and then drain. Add the lentils to the vegetables, stir and cook for about 5 minutes. Now add about 3.5 litres (14 cups) of water and bring to the boil. Turn down the heat to medium–low, add salt to taste and put a lid on the pan.

Simmer for about 45 minutes, then add the pasta and broccoli (or silverbeet) and cook until they are both soft. Serve with a drizzle of extra virgin olive oil.

(Serves 6–8)

🌺 zuppa di zucchine e patate
zucchini and potato soup

You can add pasta to this recipe to make it a full meal in itself. When the soup comes to the boil at the end of the recipe, just add a cupful of small soup pasta.

125 ml (4 fl oz/½ cup) olive oil
1 red onion, finely chopped
800–900 g (about 2 lb) zucchini (courgettes), diced
500 g (1 lb 2 oz) potatoes, peeled and diced
400 g (14 oz) tin Italian chopped tomatoes
grated parmesan cheese, to serve

Heat the oil in a saucepan over medium heat and cook the onion, zucchini and potatoes for about 5 minutes. Add the tomatoes and season with salt and pepper.

The secret of this recipe is to cook the vegetables slowly and in their own juices, so put the lid on the pan and turn the heat to low. Cook for about 30 minutes, until all the vegetables are well cooked.

Add enough water to just cover the vegetables and get a soupy consistency (if you like a thick soup, add less water; if you prefer your soup thinner, add more). Boil gently for a further 15 minutes. Season to taste and serve with a little parmesan.
(Serves 6)

zuppa di finocchio e pancetta
fennel and pancetta soup

I only use fennel when it is in season. We can buy fennel now all year round but out of season I find it too small and never as tender or flavoursome as it should be. Fennel has a male and female: the rounder ones are female; the longer ones male. Female fennel tend to be sweeter.

3–4 fennel bulbs (depending on size)
125 ml (4 fl oz/½ cup) olive oil
1 onion, finely chopped
150 g (5 oz) piece of pancetta (or bacon or prosciutto), diced
440 g (15½ oz) tin Italian chopped tomatoes
grated parmesan cheese and extra virgin olive oil, to serve

Take the outer leaves off the fennel. Cut in half and then slice each half into small pieces.

Heat the olive oil in a pot over medium heat. Add the onion and cook for about 2 minutes. Add the pancetta and cook for about 10 minutes until it starts to brown. Add the fennel and cook, stirring, for about 5 minutes.

Add the tomatoes, stir and cook for 30–40 minutes until the fennel is soft. Add enough water to just cover the fennel (probably about 2 litres/8 cups) and cook until the soup comes to the boil. Serve with parmesan and a drizzle of extra virgin olive oil.

(Serves 6)

brodo di pollo con tortellini e polpettini
tortellini in chicken soup with meatballs

1 large boiling chicken
3 carrots, cut into quarters
4 celery stalks with leaves, roughly chopped
2 onions, peeled and cut in half
stalks from ½ bunch of Italian (flat-leaf) parsley
250 g (9 oz) tortellini
grated parmesan cheese, to serve

MEATBALLS
40 g (1½ oz/½ cup) fresh breadcrumbs
3 tablespoons grated parmesan cheese
2 tablespoons chopped Italian (flat-leaf) parsley leaves
1 egg, lightly beaten

Cut the breast meat from the chicken and set aside (you can ask your butcher to help you with this if necessary). Put the whole chicken in a very large pot with the carrots, celery, onions and parsley stalks (you're using the leaves for the meatballs) and add 6–8 litres of water. Bring to the boil, reduce the heat to low, season and simmer for about 2 hours, skimming the surface occasionally to remove any froth. Cool slightly and strain the broth. I like to pick some of the chicken meat from the bones and add it to the broth, as well as a little of the celery and carrot.

Meanwhile, finely mince the chicken breast in a food processor. Add the breadcrumbs, parmesan, parsley and egg and process for about 1 minute. Transfer to a bowl and season with salt and pepper. Roll the mixture into little balls about the size of marbles, and place on a flat tray without overcrowding them.

If you're serving the brodo as a main meal, add all the meatballs. If you're serving it as a starter, freeze some of the meatballs to use another time. Bring the broth gently to the boil, then add the tortellini and cook until the pasta is halfway done, then add the meatballs for the rest of the cooking. Check the seasoning and serve with parmesan.
(Serves 6)

zuppa di borlotti
fresh borlotti bean soup

Fresh borlotti beans are available in speciality greengrocers. They take a little time to shell but you'll find it's well worth the effort. This is also lovely with some pasta added to make it more hearty. When the soup is almost ready, turn up the heat to bring it to the boil and add a cupful of small pasta. Cook until al dente.

2 kg (4½ lb) fresh borlotti beans
3 tablespoons olive oil
1 large onion, finely chopped
3 celery stalks, finely chopped
1 large carrot, finely chopped
½ fennel bulb, including fronds, finely chopped (optional)
extra virgin olive oil, to serve

Shell the beans, wash in cold water, drain and set aside. Heat the oil in a large pot over medium heat and add the onion, celery, carrot and fennel (if using). Sauté gently for about 15 minutes or until the onion is translucent. Add the beans and cook for about 5 minutes (you don't want them to brown; you just want them to sweat). Now add 2–3 litres (8–12 cups) of water, season and cook gently for about 1–1½ hours until the beans are tender.

Drizzle with extra virgin olive oil to serve.

(Serves 6)

brodo di carne con risoni

beef broth with risoni

This amount makes enough for you to be able to freeze half. I always have meat or chicken broth in the freezer for a quick meal. Just heat the broth gently until it comes to the boil and then add the pasta and cook until al dente.

3 carrots, roughly chopped
4 celery stalks, roughly chopped
2 onions, peeled and quartered
3 osso buco
2 lamb shanks
2 veal shanks
4 bay leaves
10 peppercorns
100 g (3½ oz/1 cup) risoni pasta

Preheat your oven to 200°C (400°F/Gas 6). Put the vegetables in a roasting tin, place the meat on top of the vegetables and roast in the oven for about 45 minutes. Remove them from the tin and place in a pot that's large enough to hold all the meat and vegies. Add water until it covers the meat by 5 cm (2 inches). Add the bay leaves and peppercorns, season and simmer for about 3 hours, skimming off any scum that comes to the top.

Let the stock cool and then strain. Return the stock to the clean pot. Choose some of the meat and shred it back into the stock (not too much though as this is a broth). Bring the brodo to the boil and add the pasta. Cook until al dente and then serve immediately.

(Serves 6 with enough to freeze 6 serves for another day)

pasta e piselli
pasta with peas

**This dish is so simple and cheap. Peas are the only frozen vegetable that I use —
not only are they delicious, but they make a quick and easy meal when you don't
have a lot of time. I always have a packet in the freezer. You could substitute broad
beans for the peas and cook them in the same way.**

3 tablespoons olive oil
3 spring onions (scallions), finely chopped
1 kg (2 lb 4 oz) frozen peas
500 g (1 lb 2 oz) ditalini or other small pasta
extra virgin olive oil, to serve

Heat the oil in a large saucepan over medium heat. Add the spring onions and cook for about
2 minutes until translucent.

Meanwhile, rinse the frozen peas under cold water in a colander. Add the peas to the pan, add
salt to taste and put the lid on. Turn the heat to low and cook the peas slowly, stirring occasionally.
When they start to dry out add ½ cupful of water, but not too much at once. The secret to this
recipe is to cook the peas in as little water as possible, so that they stew in their own juice. Only
add enough water to stop them sticking. Carry on like this for about 30 minutes, until the peas
are very soft, almost mushy, and sweet.

Add 3 litres (12 cups) of water and turn up the heat to high. When it comes to the boil, add
your pasta. (If you prefer more broth just add half the pasta.) I like to drizzle this with a little extra
virgin olive oil before serving.

(Serves 6)

My dress was made of the most beautiful red velvet. Mother would've made it — she was, and still is, always knitting, crocheting, sewing and painting. If she sees something she likes, she'll have a go at re-creating it herself. Many of my clothes were made by my mother or aunties: I would dream up outfits and get someone to sew them for me. I once had my auntie make me an apricot velvet dress with bell sleeves and marabou trim. I thought I looked fantastic, but I'm sure everyone else was thinking: 'there's that funny little Italian girl from down the street'.

pasta

As the world knows, the majority of Sicilians, or even Italians, have pasta in one way or another every day. Sometimes even more than once a day. We can't live without it. But we don't like too much heavy sauce on our pasta: simple and tasty, that's how we eat it.

salsa di pomodoro
simple tomato pasta sauce

I've said to cook this for about 1 hour, but I think the longer you simmer this sauce, the sweeter it becomes. With this hectic lifestyle we all lead, we tend to cook everything very quickly, which I think can take away from the flavours of the food. In the summer months, when tomatoes are in season, I use fresh tomatoes instead of tinned. Simply blanch and peel the tomatoes, chop them and add to the pan in place of the tinned ones.

125 ml (4 fl oz/½ cup) olive oil
1 large red onion, chopped
1 tablespoon chopped Italian (flat-leaf) parsley
1 tablespoon chopped basil
3 x 400 g (14 oz) tins Italian chopped tomatoes

Heat the oil in a pan and gently fry the onion until soft and almost golden. Add the herbs and stir for 30 seconds, then add the tomatoes and season with salt and pepper. Put a lid on the pan and cook over very low heat for about 1 hour, stirring occasionally. Serve with your favourite pasta. (Serves 6)

macaroni a mano
hand-made macaroni

When I was growing up, special occasions were always celebrated by the family coming together to hand-make macaroni. The women would sit around the table and roll out their dough with a long thin reed (the sort that normally grows around water). Instead of a reed, you can use a very thin knitting needle that is pointed at both ends. I remember my grandmother would plait three macaroni together and if it was your birthday you got to eat it. We don't make macaroni as much these days, which is unfortunate because it was a lot of fun sitting around the table gossiping and laughing. This is a good thing to do with family members, particularly young children. What better way to spend time together, and then share the fruits of your labour?

500 g (1 lb 2 oz) plain (all-purpose) flour
5 eggs, lightly beaten
a pinch of salt

Make the flour into a mound on your work surface and make a well in the centre, then tip the eggs and the salt into the well. With a fork, start beating the eggs and gradually mixing in some of the flour until it starts to thicken. Now with your hands mix it all together to make a ball of dough.

Knead the dough for about 10–15 minutes until it is elastic and smooth. (If it's too wet you can always add a little more flour.) Divide it in half and roll one half into a long sausage shape about 1.5 cm (¾ inch) wide. When you have a long length of dough, cut it into 3 cm (1½ inch) lengths. You have to work quickly or the dough will dry out, so only do a few at a time and keep the rest of the dough under a damp cloth while you are rolling. Lay out a clean cloth to put the macaroni on as you make them.

Lightly flour a clean smooth work surface. Place the knitting needle lengthways on top of a length of dough. Roll the needle backwards and forwards, working your hands away from the centre outwards, so the dough gradually wraps around the needle. Gently pull the knitting needle out of the macaroni and put it on the cloth. Keep rolling until you have finished all the dough.

Bring a large pot of salted water to the boil, add the macaroni and cook for 2–5 minutes depending on the size you have made them. Serve with a simple meat ragù or fresh tomato sauce and parmesan. Have fun.

(Serves 6)

ragù
tomato meat sauce

In an Italian house you would have this beautiful sauce with pasta to start the meal, and then follow with the meat and a salad. This will make a large amount of sauce but, if you're making lasagne or pasta al forno, you'll need the whole lot. If not, it freezes well or you can just halve the recipe. You don't have to use these three meats together: you can use just one or a combination.

125 ml (4 fl oz/½ cup) olive oil
1 large onion, finely chopped
1 large carrot, finely chopped
2 celery stalks, finely chopped
1 fresh pork hock
2 lamb shanks, cut in half
2 osso buco
125 ml (4 fl oz/½ cup) red wine
4 bay leaves
2.5 litres (10 cups) puréed tomatoes (tinned or bottled)

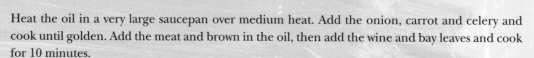

Heat the oil in a very large saucepan over medium heat. Add the onion, carrot and celery and cook until golden. Add the meat and brown in the oil, then add the wine and bay leaves and cook for 10 minutes.

Add the puréed tomatoes, season with salt and pepper and cook over low heat for 3 hours or so. The secret, I believe, to a good ragù is the long slow cooking time. The meat should just fall off the bone.

(Serves 6–8)

pasta fritta
fried leftover pasta

2–3 cupfuls leftover pasta
4 tablespoons olive oil
2 eggs, lightly beaten (optional)
2 tablespoons grated parmesan cheese

Nothing is wasted in a Sicilian home, so leftover pasta makes a great-tasting snack. It works best with tomato-based sauces. Simply heat the olive oil in a non-stick frying pan. When hot, add the pasta and stir a little. Cook for 10–15 minutes — you want the pasta to crisp up a little. Add the beaten eggs, if you're using them, wait until it sets and turn it out on to a plate. Either way, serve with a sprinkling of parmesan.

(Serves 4)

orecchiette con broccoli e acciughe

orecchiette with broccoli and anchovies

600 g (1 lb 5 oz) broccoli
125 ml (4 fl oz/½ cup) olive oil
6 anchovy fillets
3 garlic cloves, finely chopped
1 teaspoon chilli flakes (optional)
500 g (1 lb 2 oz) orecchiette pasta
grated parmesan cheese and extra virgin olive oil, to serve

Cut the broccoli into small pieces, not using too much of the stalk. Bring a large pot of salted water to the boil, add the broccoli and cook until quite soft. Scoop the broccoli out and drain, keeping the water to cook the pasta.

Heat the oil in a large non-stick frying pan and add the anchovies. Stir and cook gently until the anchovies break up, then add the garlic but don't let it brown. Add the broccoli (and chilli, if using), stir and cook for about 10 minutes, breaking up the broccoli a little as you cook it.

Meanwhile, bring the broccoli water back to the boil and cook the pasta until al dente. Drain and add to the broccoli mixture. Stir well and taste before seasoning (it may not need too much salt because of the anchovies). Sprinkle with a little parmesan and drizzle with extra virgin olive oil to serve.

(Serves 4, or 6 as a starter)

ragù di maiale e finocchio
pork and fennel ragù

Wild fennel, if you feel inspired to go hunting for it, can often be found growing along railway lines or roadsides. It looks rather like dill and is best picked in early spring, when it is young and tender. After that time the plant becomes hard and goes to seed (which is the perfect time to pick it if you're wanting to harvest the seeds). When the seeds are plump but not dry, about March or April, pick the flowers, wash them, lay them in the sun and collect them as they start to dry and fall off the stalks. You will get fennel seeds that taste far more superior to anything you can buy. If you don't have wild fennel, use half a small fennel bulb (with its tough outer layers removed) and its fronds, finely chopped. Pork and fennel sausages can be found at good Italian butchers. If you can't find them, good-quality pork sausages will do but add 2 teaspoons of fennel seeds.

4 tablespoons olive oil
1 onion, finely chopped
1 garlic clove, finely chopped
150 g (5 oz) young wild fennel, boiled for 15 minutes and chopped
6 pork and fennel sausages
3 x 400 g (14 oz) tins Italian chopped tomatoes
cooked pasta and grated parmesan cheese, to serve

Heat the olive oil in a deep frying pan or saucepan. Add the onion, garlic and chopped fennel (if you're using fennel seeds, add them now too) and sauté over medium heat for 10–15 minutes, until soft and beginning to brown.

Remove the skin from the sausages and break the meat up a little with your hands. Add to the pan, stir and break up the sausage even more with a wooden spoon. Cook until the sausage has browned (the sausage meat can be chunky if that is how you prefer it). When the meat has browned, add the tomatoes and season with salt and pepper, tasting first as some sausages are saltier than others. Reduce the heat to a simmer and cook for about 1 hour.

Serve with your favourite pasta and some grated parmesan.

(Serves 4, or 6 as a starter)

pasta con cavolfiore
pasta with cauliflower

1 small cauliflower, cut into florets
4 tablespoons olive oil
1 small red onion, finely chopped
4 anchovy fillets
1 garlic clove, finely chopped
chilli flakes (optional)
500 g (1 lb 2 oz) penne
grated parmesan or pecorino cheese, to serve

Bring a large pot of salted water to the boil, add the cauliflower and cook until you can just push a fork through it. Scoop out the cauliflower and drain, keeping the water for cooking the pasta.

Heat the oil in a large non-stick frying pan and add the onion. Cook gently until soft and just starting to brown, then add the anchovies and break them up a little with a wooden spoon. Add the garlic and cook for 2 minutes, then add the cauliflower and chilli (if using) and sauté for 5 minutes. Season to taste and set aside.

Meanwhile, cook the pasta in the cauliflower water until al dente, then drain and add the cauliflower mixture. Stir gently and taste before seasoning (it may not need too much salt because of the anchovies). Serve with a sprinkling of cheese.

(Serves 4, or 6 as a starter)

pasta con le zucchine fritte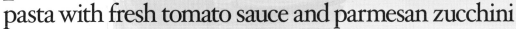
pasta with fresh tomato sauce and parmesan zucchini

FRESH TOMATO SAUCE
1 kg (2 lb 4 oz) ripe tomatoes
4 tablespoons olive oil
1 onion, finely chopped

PARMESAN ZUCCHINI
1 large zucchini (courgette)
125 ml (4 fl oz/½ cup) olive oil
50 g (1¾ oz/½ cup) grated parmesan cheese

500 g (1 lb 2 oz) spaghetti
2 tablespoons chopped basil
grated parmesan cheese, to serve

To make the tomato sauce, score a cross in the base of each tomato then blanch in boiling water for 1 minute. Put in cold water and peel the skin away from the cross. Chop the tomatoes finely.

Heat the oil in a non-stick saucepan and fry the onion over low heat until caramelised (there is nothing worse than finding raw onion in the sauce). Add the tomatoes, salt and pepper and cook slowly for about 1 hour, until the tomatoes reduce right down. I find the longer you cook the sauce, the more intense the flavour.

To make the parmesan zucchini, cut the zucchini into thin slices. Heat the oil in a non-stick frying pan, add the zucchini in a single layer, season with salt and fry until golden on one side then turn over and cook the other side. Put them on a plate and sprinkle generously with parmesan.

Cook the spaghetti in boiling salted water until al dente, then drain and stir in the tomato sauce and basil. Serve the zucchini in the middle of the table, place one or two slices on your plate and eat them along with your pasta. You could also serve the zucchini as part of an antipasto plate or as a side dish for a main course.
(Serves 4, or 6 as a starter)

✿ ragù di coniglio
rabbit ragù

125 ml (4 fl oz/½ cup) olive oil
100 g (3½ oz) piece of pancetta or bacon, diced
2 onions, finely chopped
1 small carrot, finely chopped
1 celery stalk, finely chopped
1 rabbit (wild or farmed), cut into 6–8 pieces
125 ml (4 fl oz/½ cup) white or rosé wine
4 x 400 g (14 oz) tins Italian chopped tomatoes
1 rosemary sprig
cooked pasta, to serve

Heat the oil in a large pot over medium heat. Add the pancetta and cook for about 3 minutes, then add the onions, carrot and celery and cook for about 10 minutes.

Add the rabbit to the pot and brown on all sides. When the rabbit is browned, add the wine and cook for a further 5 minutes.

Add the tomatoes, rosemary and salt and pepper and bring to the boil. Turn the heat to low and cook for 1–1½ hours until the meat starts to fall off the bone.

Lift the rabbit pieces out of the sauce and leave to cool a little. When cool enough to handle, pull the meat from the bones and return it to the sauce. You now have a beautiful ragù to serve with your favourite pasta.

(Serves 4, or 6 as a starter)

pasta al forno
baked pasta

I like to cook this sauce a day in advance and then reheat it. I find that gives it time for the flavours to deepen. If you like, you can use some mozzarella cheese in the layers as well. As a vegetarian option, use a double quantity of the simple tomato sauce on page 84, and perhaps some layers of grilled eggplant.

SAUCE

125 ml (4 fl oz/½ cup) olive oil

1 large onion, finely chopped

500 g (1 lb 2 oz) minced beef

2 lamb or veal shanks or 3 osso buco

2.5 kg (5 lb 8 oz) tinned Italian
   chopped tomatoes

300 g (10 oz) frozen peas

1 kg (2 lb 4 oz) penne

5 slices mortadella, chopped

4 hard-boiled eggs, chopped

100 g (3½ oz/1 cup) grated
   parmesan cheese

a handful of basil leaves

2 eggs, lightly beaten

To make the sauce, heat half the oil in a large saucepan and fry the onion until light golden. Add the mince, season with salt and pepper and cook, stirring, until browned.

Meanwhile, heat the rest of the oil in a frying pan and brown the shanks or osso buco on all sides, then add to the mince. Roughly purée the tomatoes in their tins and add to the pan. Add the peas and cook gently for about 2 hours until the meat falls away from the bones. Take the shanks out of the sauce, cool a little and then shred the meat off the bones. Take out 2–3 ladles of the sauce and set that aside as well.

Preheat the oven to 190°C (375°F/Gas 5). Cook the pasta in boiling salted water for a little bit shorter than the instructions (so, if the packet says 10 minutes, cook for 7 minutes, because you'll be baking it later). Drain and stir a couple of spoonfuls of sauce into the pasta to moisten it.

Spread a little sauce over the base of a deep oven dish (about 30 x 35 cm/12 x 14 inches). Arrange a layer of penne to cover the sauce. Spoon more sauce over the pasta. Add some of the shredded meat, a scattering of mortadella and egg and a generous handful of parmesan and a few basil leaves. Repeat the penne, sauce and meat layers and finish with penne on top.

Mix the eggs with the sauce you set aside earlier and spoon over the penne. Sprinkle with the last of the parmesan. Cover with foil and bake for about 40 minutes, then remove the foil and bake for a further 10–15 minutes. Rest for 15 minutes before serving.

(Serves 12)

pasta con le sarde
pasta with sardines

I like to clean the sardines myself (but if you prefer, buy them ready filleted from your fishmonger). Rinse the sardine under water to remove any scales, snap the neck bone at the back of the head with your thumb, then take out the intestines with your finger. Run your thumb down the backbone and open up the sardine. When you get to the tail, snap the bone and gently pull it away. You are now left with a butterflied sardine.

100 g (3½ oz) wild fennel, fennel fronds or dill
3 tablespoons olive oil
60 g (2 oz) dried breadcrumbs
1 red onion, finely chopped
4 anchovy fillets, chopped
12 fresh sardines, cleaned and butterflied (as above, or ask your fishmonger)

85 g (3 oz/½ cup) pine nuts, toasted
85 g (3 oz/½ cup) currants, plumped in hot water for 5 minutes
2 pinches of saffron threads, soaked in 3 tablespoons hot water
500 g (1 lb 2 oz) bucatini pasta
extra virgin olive oil, to serve

Wash the fennel and discard any dried or hard pieces. Boil the fennel or fronds in a large pot of boiling salted water (large enough to hold the pasta later) for about 10 minutes or until tender. Lift out with a slotted spoon, drain and chop finely, keeping the water.

Heat 1 tablespoon of the olive oil in a non-stick frying pan over low heat and toast the breadcrumbs, stirring constantly, until golden. Remove from the pan and set aside.

Heat the rest of the olive oil in the frying pan over medium heat and cook the onion until soft. Add the anchovies and cook for 2 minutes, then add the fennel and cook for 5–6 minutes.

Push these ingredients to the side of the pan and add the sardines (you will probably have to add them in three batches). Cook them briefly, for about 20 seconds, on each side, then push to the side and add another batch. Don't worry if they break up a little. Add the pine nuts, drained currants and saffron with the saffron water and cook gently. When it comes to the boil, turn off the heat, season and set aside.

Meanwhile, bring the pot of water back to the boil and cook the pasta until al dente. Drain and toss with the sardine sauce, then sprinkle with the breadcrumbs (this dish is meant to be dry: you may choose to only use half the amount of breadcrumbs). Drizzle with extra virgin olive oil. (Serves 4, or 6 as a starter)

cannelloni con cicoria e ricotta
cannelloni with chicory and ricotta

Chicory is available in most good greengrocers and is usually sold three to a bunch, so use all three for this dish.

1 bunch (about 800 g/1 lb 12 oz) of chicory
4 tablespoons olive oil
2 garlic cloves, finely chopped
600 g (1 lb 5 oz) fresh firm ricotta
a pinch of nutmeg
100 g (3½ oz/1 cup) grated parmesan cheese
1 quantity tomato pasta sauce (page 84)
250 g (9 oz) fresh lasagne sheets

Bring a large pot of salted water to the boil. Discard the very ends of the chicory and slice thinly (about 2 cm/¾ inch). Wash the chicory in cold water a couple of times to get rid of any grit, then blanch in the boiling water for 5–10 minutes and drain.

Heat the oil in a frying pan over medium heat. Add the garlic and cook for 30 seconds. Add the chicory, season and cook for about 10–15 minutes until tender. Leave to cool completely.

Put the ricotta in a bowl and mash with a fork. Add the nutmeg and half the parmesan, and salt and pepper and mix well. Add the cooled chicory and mix again. Cut the lasagne sheets into 12 cm (5 inch) rectangles and preheat the oven to 180°C (350°F/Gas 4).

Warm the tomato sauce in a pan for a few minutes until hot. Lay about half the tomato sauce in a large oven dish. Take 2 tablespoons of the ricotta mixture and place at one end of a pasta rectangle and then roll up. Place in the oven dish, join side down. Repeat until you have used all the pasta sheets and filling.

Cover the cannelloni with the remaining tomato sauce and parmesan. Cover with baking paper, then foil, seal the edges tightly and bake in the oven for 1 hour.
(Serves 6)

pesto siciliano
sicilian pesto

6 ripe tomatoes
100 g (3½ oz) blanched almonds
2 garlic cloves
leaves from 1 large bunch of basil
leaves from ½ bunch of Italian (flat-leaf) parsley
leaves from ½ bunch of mint
185 ml (6 fl oz/¾ cup) olive oil
2 teaspoons chilli flakes
500 g (1 lb 2 oz) spaghetti
50 g (1¾ oz/½ cup) grated parmesan cheese

Score a cross in the base of each tomato then blanch in boiling water for 1 minute. Put into cold water and peel the skin away from the cross. Chop the tomatoes finely, removing the seeds. Finely grind the almonds in a food processor. Add the garlic, herbs and oil and process to a fine paste, then transfer to a bowl.

Add the tomatoes to the processor and pulse a few times until roughly chopped. Add to the pesto mixture with the chilli flakes and some salt and pepper and mix thoroughly.

Cook the spaghetti in a large pot of boiling salted water until al dente. Drain and toss with the pesto and parmesan. Check the seasoning before serving with more parmesan. If the dish is a little dry, add a drizzle of extra virgin olive oil before serving.
(Serves 4, or 6 as a starter)

spaghetti al nero di seppia
spaghetti with squid in black ink sauce

When you clean the squid, be careful to preserve the ink sac. Or, if you prefer, buy the squid ink in sachets and use ready-cleaned squid instead.

500 g (1 lb 2 oz) squid, including ink sacs
4 tablespoons olive oil
1 red onion, finely chopped
2 garlic cloves, finely chopped
400 g (14 oz) tin Italian chopped tomatoes
500 g (1 lb 2 oz) spaghetti
2 tablespoons chopped Italian (flat-leaf) parsley

To clean the squid, separate the tentacles from the body by pulling on them gently; you should pull out the insides of the squid attached to the tentacles, being careful to save the ink sac. Cut the tentacles just below the eyes. Keep the tentacles and discard the rest. Run your hand inside the body and pull out the thin clear bone inside. Rinse the insides well. Pull the wings from the sides and set aside.

Under gently running water pull the skin from the body and wings of the squid. It should pull away easily or you may choose to place it on a board and scrape the skin off with a knife, then rinse under running water. There is no need to remove the skin from the tentacles, just rinse well in cold water and run your hand firmly down the tentacles to remove any sharp parts. Drain and pat dry. Chop the squid into thin strips and the tentacles into small pieces, then dry as thoroughly as possible with a tea towel.

Heat the oil in a large pan and fry the onion until golden. Add the garlic and cook for about 1 minute, then add the squid and cook, stirring, over medium heat for about 15 minutes or until it starts to turn golden. Add a touch of water if the squid starts to stick. Now add the tomatoes and some salt and pepper. Cover the pan and turn the heat down to low. Simmer for about 40 minutes, stirring occasionally. Stir in the ink and simmer for another 10 minutes.

Meanwhile, cook the pasta in a large pot of boiling salted water until al dente. Drain, toss with the sauce, sprinkle with parsley and serve. This sauce is quite lovely even without the ink. (Serves 4, or 6 as a starter)

penne con pomodori fresci
penne with fresh tomato

This is one of those easy dishes that I often prepare when I'm in a hurry or can't be bothered cooking. It takes no time at all...

500 g (1 lb 2 oz) penne
4 tablespoons olive oil
3 garlic cloves, finely chopped
4 ripe tomatoes, diced
1 teaspoon chilli flakes
3 tablespoons finely chopped Italian (flat-leaf) parsley
3 tablespoons extra virgin olive oil
grated parmesan cheese, to serve

Cook the pasta in a large pot of boiling salted water until al dente. Meanwhile, heat the olive oil in a frying pan over medium heat and cook the garlic for 1 minute. Add the tomatoes and chilli flakes and cook for about 5 minutes.

Drain the pasta and toss with the tomatoes, parsley and extra virgin olive oil. Serve with a little parmesan. See? Quick and easy.

(Serves 4, or 6 as a starter)

spaghetti con mollica e cipolline
spaghetti with breadcrumbs and spring onions

I'm not sure where this recipe comes from, but it is certainly something born out of necessity. Nothing in the cupboard but stale bread, and some onions in the garden... let's make a sauce.

250 ml (9 fl oz/1 cup) olive oil
250 g (9 oz/2½ cups) dry breadcrumbs
1 garlic clove, finely chopped
1 bunch spring onions (scallions), chopped
500 g (1 lb 2 oz) spaghetti
50 g (1¾ oz/½ cup) grated parmesan cheese
125 ml (4 fl oz/½ cup) extra virgin olive oil

Heat half the olive oil in a frying pan over medium heat. Add the breadcrumbs and fry gently: they should swell a little as they absorb the oil. Season with salt and pepper. Add the garlic and cook for a couple of minutes, then tip out onto a plate and set aside.

Pour the rest of the olive oil into the cleaned pan over medium heat. Add the spring onions and cook for about 5 minutes. Turn the heat down to low and cook for about 20 minutes.

Meanwhile, cook the pasta in a large pot of boiling salted water until al dente. Drain, return to the pot and add the onions, breadcrumbs and parmesan. Stir well and drizzle with the extra virgin olive oil. Serve hot.

(Serves 4, or 6 as a starter)

pasta e ricotta
pasta with ricotta

**Why get take-away when you can have something so simple and quick?
This pasta dish can be changed in many ways:**
- **Add 2 tablespoons olive oil, 3 tablespoons grated parmesan
  and 1 tablespoon chopped parsley.**
- **Add 2 tablespoons pesto and 3 tablespoons grated parmesan.**
- **Add 2 diced ripe tomatoes and a handful of chopped basil.**
- **Add a few chopped cooked bacon rashers and some cooked peas
  and 3 tablespoons grated parmesan.**

But I still love it with just ricotta.

> **500 g (1 lb 2 oz) shell pasta**
> **250 g (9 oz) fresh firm ricotta**
> **a bit of chopped Italian (flat-leaf) parsley**

Cook the pasta in a large pot of boiling salted water until al dente. Meanwhile, mash the ricotta with a fork and set aside.

Drain the pasta, keeping a little of the cooking water. Add the ricotta to the pasta, and as much of the cooking water as you need to loosen it up. Stir together well, add the parsley, season with salt and pepper and serve.

(Serves 4, or 6 as a starter)

Sicilians are obsessed with hunting (so much so that it is hard to imagine there are many animals left in the wild). This photo was taken on one of the many trips we made back to my parents' home villages. They were close to each other, so we would visit my father's family, then his father would lead us over to my mother's village with me riding on his donkey. Here we had obviously stopped halfway, probably for my grandfather to bag a wild rabbit for dinner.

casalinga and ricotta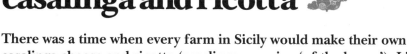

There was a time when every farm in Sicily would make their own casalinga cheese and ricotta (casalinga meaning 'of the house'). Like making salami, this is a team effort; we enjoy doing things together and at the same time passing on the traditions. My mother is passionate about ricotta and on one of my parents' trips to Sicily, she somehow brought back a monster cauldron and all the wicker baskets required for the traditional method.

When my mother visits us at our farm we seek out some whole milk and start having fun. It's a long fiddly process, done without a written recipe or measurements. My mother would say it's all about the experience and the 'feel'. The milk is heated over an open fire until Mum can no longer stand to leave her hand in there (this is kitchen chemistry). The rennet is added and left to stand. The curds are brought together and lifted into wicker baskets, pressed, rotated and pressed again to form the cheese. We then place the whey and some extra milk back on the fire and cook again for Italian ricotta.

My father's village of Basico is well regarded as making great ricotta. It still allows locals to bring in their own small amount of sheep's milk and make ricotta co-operatively. The 'cheat's' recipe that follows is a simple way to get a good result at home. Ricotta can be sun-dried to make a creamy caramel grating cheese for serving over pasta.

 # ricotta

4 litres (16 cups) whole milk
185 ml (6 fl oz/¾ cup) cream
2 teaspoons salt
1 teaspoon liquid rennet (available from chemists)

Heat the milk and cream to 200°C (400°F), then pour into another pot (this will help with the cooling). Add the salt and stir until it has dissolved. Put the pot into a sink of iced water and then keep checking the temperature with a cooking thermometer until the milk has cooled to about 125°C (255°F).

Mix the rennet with about 3 tablespoons water, then stir into the milk. Leave now without touching for about 10–15 minutes for the milk to thicken.

Make 2 cuts on top of the solids then stir quickly for 20 seconds to break it all up. Gently stir around the edge with a wooden spoon. The ricotta should now start to separate from the whey. With a large slotted spoon, gently scoop out the ricotta into a colander or ricotta moulds and leave it to stand for about 2 hours before refrigerating. It should keep for up to 4 days.

This was Zia Caterina's wedding and I was so excited because I was asked to be a flower girl. It was a fairly small wedding — only 150 people. When any of my cousins get married now there are usually about 400 guests. Sicilian weddings are all about the food: antipasti, pasta, a main course, fruit, dessert… and when you finally think it's over, out comes the supper. Luckily there is always a lot of dancing to help the food go down.

carne e pesce

Growing up in a fairly inaccessible Sicilian hill village, I have only faint memories of fish! But if you lived on the coast, seafood was the starting point for some of Sicily's most celebrated dishes. We usually raised and slaughtered our own farm animals, but only for special occasions. The whole animal would be eaten (Sicilians don't believe in waste).

capretto con castagne
kid with chestnuts

Capretto (kid) is usually available already chopped from your butcher, although you might need to order it specially. I prefer the leg end, but the shoulder is probably just as good. If you can't find kid, use lamb instead. Dried chestnuts are available in good Italian delis and nut shops.

20 dried chestnuts
150 g (5 oz/1 cup) plain (all-purpose) flour
2 kg (4½ lb) capretto, cut into small pieces
185 ml (6 fl oz/¾ cup) olive oil
1 large onion, finely chopped
3 celery stalks, thinly sliced
1 litre (35 fl oz/4 cups) chicken or beef stock
1 rosemary sprig

Soak the dried chestnuts in water overnight and then drain.

Heat the oven to 180°C (350°F/Gas 4). Season the flour with salt and pepper and use to lightly dust the capretto. Heat ½ cup of the olive oil in a frying pan and brown the capretto pieces, then transfer to an oven dish.

Clean the frying pan and add the remaining oil over medium heat. Fry the onion and celery until slightly golden, then tip into the oven dish. Pour in the stock and add the rosemary and chestnuts. Season with salt and pepper, seal the dish tightly with foil or a lid and bake for 1½ hours. Remove the foil and bake for another 30 minutes, turning the meat once.

(Serves 6)

pollo con olive e caperi
chicken with olives and capers

250 ml (9 fl oz/1 cup) olive oil

6 chicken marylands (leg and thigh pieces on the bone)

1 large red onion, finely chopped

90 g (3 oz/½ cup) small salted capers, rinsed

100 g (3½ oz/½ cup) pitted green olives

250 ml (9 fl oz/1 cup) white wine

4 tomatoes, diced

500 ml (17 fl oz/2 cups) chicken stock

Heat the oven to 180°C (350°F/Gas 4). Heat half the oil in a large frying pan and brown the chicken until golden on all sides — you will probably need to do this in two batches, depending on the size of your pan.

Heat the rest of the oil in a flameproof casserole that is big enough to later hold all the chicken, and fry the onion until starting to brown. Add the capers and olives and cook for 3–4 minutes, then add the browned chicken and cook for a further 2 minutes. Add the wine and let it come to the boil for 2 minutes, then stir in the tomatoes and stock.

Cover the casserole with a lid or foil and bake for 1 hour. Uncover and cook for another 15 minutes.

(Serves 6)

bistecca al salmoriglio

steak with olive oil and lemon dressing

I have said Scotch fillet but you can choose any cut of meat here, such as lamb cutlets, beef eye fillets or chicken fillets, thinly sliced — the meat is irrelevant; this dish is all about the salmoriglio! You can cook this on a barbecue or a hot chargrill on the stove. It's equally great for a large outdoor gathering, or dinner for one. I usually serve it with a salad and fried potatoes.

250 ml (9 fl oz/1 cup) olive oil, plus a little extra for cooking
125 ml (4 fl oz/½ cup) lemon juice
3 garlic cloves, peeled and left whole but lightly crushed
1 tablespoon dried oregano
12 pieces Scotch fillet, thinly sliced by your butcher

To make the salmoriglio, mix together the oil, lemon juice, garlic and oregano and season with salt and pepper. Brush the meat with the extra olive oil, then season with salt and pepper. Heat the barbecue or chargrill to very hot, and cook the steak for only a few minutes on each side, depending on how well you like it done.

As soon as the steak is cooked, dip it into the salmoriglio and serve at once.

(Serves 6)

coniglio agro dolce
sweet and sour rabbit

Order wild rabbit from your butcher if possible. When you cut the rabbits into pieces, you might want to discard the ribcage — I don't use it as I find it breaks up too much, leaving too many bones.

2 young rabbits, cut into 6–8 pieces
150 g (5 oz/1 cup) plain (all-purpose) flour
125 ml (4 fl oz/½ cup) olive oil
1 onion, thinly sliced
1 celery stalk, finely chopped
1 small carrot, finely chopped
2 tablespoons small salted capers, rinsed
3 tablespoons sultanas, plumped in water for about 5 minutes
200 g (7 oz/1 cup) large pitted green olives, roughly chopped
4 tablespoons honey
125 ml (4 fl oz/½ cup) red wine vinegar
750 ml (26 fl oz/3 cups) chicken stock

Preheat the oven to 160°C (315°F/Gas 2–3). Lightly coat the rabbit with the flour, seasoned with salt and pepper. Heat the oil in a large non-stick frying pan, add the rabbit in batches and brown all over. Remove all the rabbit from the pan.

Add the onion, celery and carrot to the pan and cook for about 10 minutes over medium heat. Add the capers, sultanas and olives and cook, stirring, for about 5 minutes.

Put the rabbit pieces in a large roasting tin and tip the onion mixture over the rabbit. Mix together the honey and vinegar and, when the honey has dissolved, pour over the rabbit. Add the stock and season with salt and pepper.

Cover tightly with foil and bake for 1–2 hours, checking the rabbit every 30 minutes. I cook a lot of rabbit and have found that they vary greatly as to how long they need to cook; perhaps a seasonal thing. When the meat starts to fall off the bone, the dish is ready.

(Serves 6–8)

vitello al marsala
veal marsala

This is a very traditional Sicilian dish whose reputation has been spoilt by many very bad versions, usually containing too much cream or Marsala. In its pure form this is a very simple, quick dish.

2 tablespoons olive oil
25 g (1 oz) butter
12 slices veal
100 ml (3½ fl oz) Marsala
125 ml (4 fl oz/½ cup) cream

Heat half the oil and half the butter in a large frying pan and, when the butter starts to bubble and the pan is very hot, add 6 slices of veal (the veal needs to cook very quickly so it doesn't stew). Cook for 1 minute on each side, then remove from the pan and use the remaining oil and butter to cook the rest of the veal. Remove all the veal to a plate.

Add the Marsala to the frying pan and cook, stirring, for about 1 minute. Add the cream and cook for about 30 seconds. Bring the veal back to the pan and turn once in the sauce to make sure it is warm.

(Serves 6)

cotoletta
crumbed chicken

Go into any Sicilian home, open the fridge and I can guarantee there will be a plate of cotoletta in there somewhere. Sicilians love their cotoletta very thin, and the ingredients vary as everyone has their own recipe. Cotoletta can be chicken, veal or beef — I like chicken best of all. We also eat this, while it's still warm, in a roll with a little lettuce.

200 g (7 oz/2 cups) dry breadcrumbs
100 g (3½ oz/1 cup) grated parmesan cheese
3 tablespoons finely chopped Italian (flat-leaf) parsley
1 garlic clove, very finely chopped
3 eggs, lightly beaten
3–4 chicken breast fillets, very thinly sliced
olive oil, for frying

Mix together the breadcrumbs, parmesan, parsley, garlic and some salt and pepper in a large flat bowl. Put the beaten eggs in another bowl.

Dip the chicken into the egg, then into the breadcrumb mixture. Cover the chicken with the breadcrumbs, pressing so it is all well covered.

Heat enough oil to cover the bottom of a frying pan. Fry the cotoletta in the oil, turning when they are golden (you may need to cook them in batches, depending on the size of your pan). Drain on kitchen paper before serving.

(Serves 6)

baccalà

Baccalà (salt cod) takes a bit of forward planning. When you buy it in a deli, ask them to chop it into smaller pieces for you. Then you need to soak the baccalà in cold water for three days, changing the water regularly three times a day. When you've done this, drain the baccalà on a tea towel to soak up the excess water.

125 ml (4 fl oz/½ cup) olive oil
1 onion, finely chopped
500 g (1 lb 2 oz) ripe tomatoes, peeled, seeded and chopped or
    440 g (15½ oz) tin Italian chopped tomatoes
1 kg (2 lb 4 oz) baccalà (salt cod), soaked in cold water for 3 days, as above
150 g (5 oz) pitted green olives
3 large potatoes, peeled and quartered

Preheat the oven to 180°C (350°F/Gas 4). Heat the olive oil over medium heat in a flameproof casserole (that is big enough to later hold all the fish in a single layer). Add the onion and cook until soft, then add the tomatoes and cook for about 15 minutes.

Add the baccalà to the casserole, with the olives and potatoes and spread it all out evenly. Add 500 ml (17 fl oz/2 cups) of water, season with pepper (no need for salt!), cover and bake for about 45 minutes, turning the baccalà halfway through. If it looks too dry, add a little more water. When it's ready the baccalà should easily flake away from the bone. Serve with lots of bread to soak up the sauce.

(Serves 6)

farsomagro
stuffed sicilian beef roll

This is a traditional Sicilian favourite — every family has its own version. You could also make miniature versions with thin slices of topside beef and quail eggs, perhaps for a dinner party.

1.5 kg (3 lb 5 oz) girello roast or piece of
    beef shoulder, boned by your butcher
    and flattened as much as possible so
    that you can roll it easily
2 tablespoons grated parmesan cheese
5 slices mortadella
large leaves from ½ bunch of spinach
6 hard-boiled eggs, peeled but left whole
125 ml (4 fl oz/½ cup) olive oil

FOR THE SAUCE
3 tablespoons olive oil
1 large onion, finely chopped
1 small celery stalk, finely chopped
1 small carrot, finely chopped
2.5 kg (5 lb 8 oz) tin or 4 x 500 ml
    (17 fl oz) bottles of puréed tomatoes
2 bay leaves

To make the sauce, heat the oil in a large saucepan that is big enough to later hold all the meat. Cook the onion, celery and carrot over low heat until golden, then add the tomato purée and bay leaves, season with salt and pepper and leave to simmer while you prepare the meat.

Lay the meat on a flat surface, season with salt and pepper and sprinkle with the parmesan. Lay the slices of mortadella down the centre of the meat (it's ok if they overlap). Lay the spinach leaves over the mortadella. Arrange the eggs lengthways in a line down the centre of the meat. Season again with salt and pepper.

Now comes the tricky part: rolling it all up. Start to roll from one long side, tying with kitchen string at intervals of about 8 cm (3 inches). Make sure the ends are tied very tightly or you will lose the eggs.

Heat the oil in a large frying pan and brown the farsomagro on all sides, then add to the sauce in the pan. Cover the pan and cook over very low heat for 1–1½ hours, turning occasionally. Remove from the sauce and leave to cool slightly. Remove the string before slicing. Spoon some of the sauce onto a large serving plate then arrange the slices on top and serve.
(Serves 8)

🌺 involtini
beef rolls stuffed with breadcrumbs and prosciutto

160 g (5½ oz/2 cups) fresh white breadcrumbs
3 tablespoons chopped Italian (flat-leaf) parsley
1 garlic clove, finely chopped
50 g (1¾ oz/½ cup) grated parmesan cheese
1 egg, lightly beaten
12 slices beef topside, sliced very thinly
6 slices prosciutto, cut in half
125 ml (4 fl oz/½ cup) olive oil
1 red onion, finely chopped
3 x 400 g (14 oz) tins Italian chopped tomatoes

Mix together the breadcrumbs, parsley, garlic, parmesan and some salt and pepper. Add the beaten egg and mix well with your hands. Add a little water, if needed, to just bring it together.

Lay the slices of beef on a work surface and top with half a slice of prosciutto. Take a small handful of the breadcrumb mixture, roll it a little in your hand, then place at the narrow end of the meat slice. Roll up the slice of meat to enclose the filling, tucking in the sides as you do. Secure with a toothpick and set aside while you make the rest.

Heat half the oil in a saucepan that is large enough to later hold all the involtini. Add the onion and fry until golden, then add the tomatoes. Season and turn the heat down to low.

Meanwhile, heat the remaining oil in a frying pan and brown the involtini on all sides. Add to the pan with the sauce, put a lid on the pan and simmer for about 40 minutes.
(Serves 6)

lumache con pomodoro
snails in tomato sauce

When I was younger and my grandfather was alive he had the most magnificent vegetable garden. He never used any pesticides so when it rained we would all go outside and find as many snails as we could. They were just regular garden snails but they tasted wonderful in this sauce. I'm not sure whether it is still possible to collect snails in gardens now, but if you live in the country and don't use pesticides you should be able to gather your own. If not, there are people now breeding snails for cooking.

1–1.5 kg (2½ –3½ lb) snails in their shells
125 ml (4 fl oz/½ cup) olive oil
1 onion, finely chopped
2 garlic cloves, finely chopped
440 g (15½ oz) tin Italian chopped tomatoes
2 tablespoons chopped Italian (flat-leaf) parsley
2 large potatoes, peeled and each cut into 3–4 pieces

When you've collected the snails they must be purged of grit and dirt by putting them in a plastic bucket with bran for a few days (if you've bought them they should just be washed and drained).

Heat the oil in a frying pan and cook the onion gently until just turning golden. Add the garlic and cook for about 1 minute, then add the tomatoes, snails, parsley and potatoes. Season, then cover the pan and cook gently for about 40–50 minutes.

Serve with good crusty bread and a strong toothpick to remove the snails from their shells. (Serves 6)

tonno agro dolce
sweet and sour tuna

6 tuna steaks (not too thick)
75 g (2½ oz/½ cup) plain (all-purpose) flour
125 ml (4 fl oz/½ cup) olive oil
1 large red onion, thinly sliced
50 g (1¾ oz) currants, plumped in water for 10 minutes
100 g (3½ oz/½ cup) chopped green olives
3 tablespoons dry Marsala
2 tablespoons sugar
125 ml (4 fl oz/½ cup) red wine vinegar

Coat the fish lightly in the flour and shake off any excess. Heat half the olive oil in a large frying pan over medium heat and cook the onion until soft and translucent. Remove from the pan.

Heat the remaining oil in the pan, add the fish (you'll probably need to cook it in two batches) and cook for 3–4 minutes on each side, depending on its thickness. Add the onions, currants, olives, Marsala and the sugar mixed with the vinegar. Turn the heat down to low and cook gently for 5 minutes. Season with salt and pepper before serving.

(Serves 6)

calamari alla griglia
grilled calamari

6 squid, each about 20 cm (8 inches) long
125 ml (4 fl oz/½ cup) extra virgin olive oil
3 tablespoons lemon juice
3 tablespoons chopped Italian (flat-leaf) parsley
2 garlic cloves, roughly chopped
chilli flakes (optional)

To clean the squid, separate the tentacles from the body by pulling on them gently; you should pull out the insides of the squid attached to the tentacles. Cut the tentacles just below the eyes. Keep the tentacles and discard the rest. Run your hand inside the body and pull out the thin clear bone inside. Rinse the insides well. Pull the wings from the sides and set aside.

Under gently running water pull the skin from the body and wings of the squid. It should pull away easily or you may choose to place the squid on a board and scrape the skin off with a knife, then rinse under running water.

There is no need to remove the skin from the tentacles, just rinse well in cold water and run your hand firmly down the tentacles to remove any sharp parts. Drain and pat the squid pieces dry. Now you are ready.

Mix the oil, lemon juice, parsley, garlic and chilli, if using, in a large bowl. Season with salt and pepper, add the squid and mix well. Cover with plastic wrap and refrigerate for at least 3 hours.

Heat a barbecue or chargrill plate and add the squid pieces and tentacles — if your chargrill is small you may have to cook in two batches. You need to flatten the pieces on the barbecue so they will cook on the inside — I like to place a baking tray on top of them and then put a heavy saucepan on top of the tray to weigh it down. Cook the squid for 5 minutes, then turn over and cook for another 5 minutes. Cut into 2 cm (¾ inch) calamari rings to serve. Good with a squeeze of lemon.

(Serves 6)

polpette
meatballs in tomato sauce

In an Italian home this would become two meals: the sauce would be served on pasta and then the meatballs eaten as a main course with salad. Also you can make small meatballs and fry them for a little longer to make wonderful party food. They also freeze well — thaw and cook in the oven for about 15 minutes.

1 kg (2 lb 4 oz) coarsely minced topside beef
500 g (1 lb 2 oz) minced pork
160 g (5½ oz/2 cups) fresh white breadcrumbs
150 g (5 oz/1½ cups) grated parmesan cheese
1 garlic clove, finely chopped
3 tablespoons chopped Italian (flat-leaf) parsley
4 eggs
185 ml (4 fl oz/¾ cup) olive oil
2 onions, finely chopped
2.5 kg (5 lb 8 oz) tinned Italian chopped tomatoes
2 bay leaves

Mix together the meat, breadcrumbs, parmesan, garlic, parsley and some salt and pepper (use your hands for this). Add 3 lightly beaten eggs and again mix well. The mixture should all come together — if it feels too dry, add a little of the fourth egg but don't make it too wet or the meatballs will fall apart. (To check, take a handful of mixture and roll it into a ball; if it all comes together and is firm, you've got it right.)

Start rolling the mixture into balls. The size is up to you, just make sure they are rolled firmly so they keep their shape.

Heat 4 tablespoons of the oil in a pan that is large enough to later hold all the meatballs. Fry the onions until quite soft, then add the tomatoes and cook over low heat, stirring occasionally.

Heat the rest of the oil in a non-stick frying pan and add some of the meatballs, but don't overcrowd them. Brown them on all sides until golden brown (it should only take 1–2 minutes on each side). As they are browned, lift them out and add to the pan of tomato sauce. When you've added all the meatballs to the sauce, add the bay leaves, season, cover and simmer for about 1 hour.

(Serves 6)

trippa
tripe

Tripe: you either love it or you hate it. I just wish more people would try it.

    1.5 kg (3 lb 5 oz) tripe
    3 tablespoons olive oil
    1 onion, finely chopped
    1 small carrot, finely chopped
    1 celery stalk, finely chopped
    250 ml (9 fl oz/1 cup) white wine
    440 g (15½ oz) tin Italian chopped tomatoes
    1 litre (35 fl oz/4 cups) chicken stock
    2 tablespoons Italian (flat-leaf) parsley
    1 large rosemary sprig
    1 teaspoon chilli flakes
    3 potatoes (spunta are good), peeled and cut into quarters
    400 g (14 oz) tin lima beans
    grated parmesan cheese, to serve

Cut the tripe into strips. Heat the oil in a large saucepan and cook the onion, carrot and celery until soft. Add the tripe and cook for about 10 minutes, stirring so it doesn't stick. Add the wine and cook for another 10 minutes. Add the tomatoes, chicken stock, parsley, rosemary, chilli flakes and salt and pepper to taste.

Cover the pan and cook for 2 hours, checking often as it cooks; you want the tripe to be soft but with a bit of bite. If the mixture becomes too dry, add a little more chicken stock or water.

After the 2 hours, add the potatoes and cook until soft. Add the beans and cook for another 10 minutes. Sprinkle with parmesan and serve with crusty bread to soak up the juices.
(Serves 6)

porchetta

Traditionally, porchetta is the whole pig which is boned and stuffed, then roasted. I like to serve this with baked fennel and salad. But it is great cold in a roll, too.

125 ml (4 fl oz/½ cup) olive oil
1 onion, finely chopped
1 small fennel, finely chopped, or a handful of wild fennel
250 g (9 oz) minced pork
3 garlic cloves, crushed
1 tablespoon ground black pepper
3 tablespoons chopped rosemary
1 tablespoon fennel seeds, pounded with a mortar and pestle
1 leg of pork (about 3 kg/6 lb 12 oz), boned and butterflied

Preheat the oven to 250°C (500°F/Gas 9). Heat the oil in a large frying pan over medium heat, add the onion and fennel and cook for about 10 minutes. Add the minced pork and cook for another 15 minutes. Now add the garlic, pepper, rosemary and fennel seeds. Season with salt, stir and turn off the heat.

Lay the leg of pork on a flat surface, opening it out as much as possible so it will be easier to roll. Place the filling down the centre and spread it out a little, but not too close to the edges. Roll up the pork and tie as tight as possible with kitchen string. Score the skin with a sharp knife and rub it with a little olive oil and salt.

Put the pork in a roasting tin and add 185 ml (6 fl oz/¾ cup) of water. Bake for 15 minutes, then turn the oven down to 190°C (375°F/Gas 5) and cook for 1½ to 2 hours, depending on the size. Rest for 30 minutes before slicing to serve.
(Serves 6–8 with leftovers for lunch the next day)

calamari ripieni
stuffed calamari

If you like, you can double the amount of sauce here and serve the sauce with pasta as a starter and then the squid with salad for the main — the Italian way.

It is important to buy fresh squid and not the calamari tubes that are readily available (I find these very inferior in quality). Your fishmonger will clean the squid if you want but it's very easy: have a go following these simple steps.

6 squid, each about 15 cm (6 inches) long, or 3 larger squid
185 ml (6 fl oz/¾ cup) olive oil
2 leeks, white part only, finely sliced
1 red onion, finely chopped
2 garlic cloves, finely chopped
160 g (5½ oz/2 cups) fresh white breadcrumbs
2 tablespoons small salted capers, rinsed
1 egg, lightly beaten
3 tablespoons grated parmesan cheese
3 tablespoons chopped Italian (flat-leaf) parsley
125 ml (4 fl oz/½ cup) white wine
400 g (14 oz) tin Italian chopped tomatoes

To clean the squid, separate the tentacles from the body by pulling on them gently; you should pull out the insides of the squid attached to the tentacles. Cut the tentacles just below the eyes. Keep the tentacles and discard the rest. Run your hand inside the body and pull out the thin clear bone inside. Rinse the insides well. Pull the wings from the sides and set aside.

Under running water pull the skin from the body and wings of the squid. It should pull away easily or you can scrape it off with a knife, then rinse under running water.

There is no need to remove the skin from the tentacles, just rinse well in cold water and run your hand firmly down the tentacles to remove any sharp parts. Drain and pat the squid tubes dry. Now you are ready.

Chop the tentacles and wings very finely and set aside. Heat 3 tablespoons of the olive oil in a pan over medium heat, add the leek and onion and cook for 5 minutes. Add the chopped squid and 1 clove of garlic. Turn the heat down a little and cook for about 15–20 minutes, stirring constantly. Turn off the heat and add the breadcrumbs and capers, stir well and set aside to cool for about an hour. Add the egg, parmesan, parsley and salt and pepper to taste, being mindful that the capers will be salty. Mix well.

Use a spoon to stuff the body of the squid with the mixture. Do not fill them too full, about three-quarters is fine, as they will shrink when cooked. Close the top of the squid with a skewer or toothpick.

Choose a large pan that will fit all the squid in a single layer. Heat the remaining olive oil and brown the squid all over. Turn the heat to medium, add the white wine and cook for 2–3 minutes, turning the squid once or twice. Add the tomatoes and remaining garlic and season with salt and pepper. Turn the heat down to low, cover and cook for 40–50 minutes, depending on the size of the squid. Turn them occasionally during cooking and if the sauce dries out add a little water. The squid are done when they feel tender if pricked with a fork. Slice them and spoon a little of the sauce over each one.

(Serves 6)

swordfish al salmoriglio
swordfish with olive oil and lemon dressing

250 ml (9 fl oz/1 cup) extra virgin olive oil
1 garlic clove, peeled and left whole but lightly crushed
2 tablespoons chopped Italian (flat-leaf) parsley
2 tablespoons chopped mint
juice of 2 lemons
6 swordfish fillets, or other firm white fish

Mix together the oil, garlic, parsley, mint and lemon juice and season well. Take out a quarter of the salmoriglio to use for dressing later. Put the fish in the marinade and leave for about 1 hour.

The fish can be cooked on a barbecue, in a non-stick frying pan, or on a chargrill pan — any method is fine as long as it is very hot. Cook the fish for about 2–3 minutes on each side (depending on thickness) until cooked through. Serve at once with a drizzle of salmoriglio.
(Serves 6)

sarde al beccafico
stuffed sardines

You can serve these as a main course with a salad, but they also make a lovely pre-dinner snack.

24 fresh sardines
160 g (5½ oz/2 cups) fresh white breadcrumbs
1 small garlic clove, finely chopped
1 handful of chopped Italian (flat-leaf) parsley
50 g (1¾ oz/½ cup) grated parmesan cheese
1 egg, lightly beaten
125 ml (4 fl oz/½ cup) olive oil
100 g (3½ oz/⅔ cup) plain (all-purpose) flour

I like to buy the sardines and clean them myself (but if you prefer you can buy them already filleted from your fishmonger). Rinse the sardine under running water to remove any scales, snap the neck bone at the back of the head with your thumb, then take out the intestines with your finger. Now run your thumb down the backbone as if using a knife and simply open up the sardine. When you get to the tail, snap the bone with your fingers or scissors, then gently pull the bone away. You are now left with a butterflied sardine. Repeat until all your sardines are butterflied.

Mix together the breadcrumbs, garlic, parsley, parmesan, egg and some salt and pepper, adding a little bit of water if necessary to just moisten it. Place a butterflied sardine in the palm of your hand, skin side down. Take a small amount of the breadcrumb mixture (about 1 tablespoon), place in the middle of the sardine and flatten down the centre, leaving the edges free of mixture. Put another sardine on top, skin side up, and press together gently. Repeat until all the sardines are stuffed.

Heat half the oil in a large non-stick frying pan over medium heat. Meanwhile, put the flour in a flat bowl, season with salt and pepper and use to lightly flour the sardines. Fry the sardines in batches for 4–5 minutes or until golden brown (don't fry them too quickly or the centres won't cook) then turn over and cook the other side until golden. Season with salt and move to a plate as they're cooked. You'll need to top up the oil in the pan as you go.
(Serves 4)

This is me and Aldo, my youngest brother, in the garden at Nonno's. They had a large house, and an even larger garden. There was not one inch that wasn't planted with something: broad beans and zucchini, figs and tomatoes, grapevines... They even had chickens running around. Fortunately, there was a big front yard for the children to play in, because there was certainly no room for us out the back. Nonno and Nonna had eleven offspring, so, with partners and children, we were usually 25 for dinner. One of my uncles is a carpenter and made a special table for us.

verdura

Traditionally, vegetables were cooked more often in a Sicilian kitchen than was meat. Meat was expensive and so was saved for special occasions and celebrations. In my parents' villages vegetables were harvested in summer and preserved for the winter months when snow covered the ground.

finocchio gratinato
baked fennel

1 large or 2 small fennel bulbs with fronds and stems
3 tablespoons olive oil
1 garlic clove, finely chopped
50 g (1¾ oz/½ cup) grated parmesan cheese

Cut the fronds from the fennel. Remove the outer leaves of the fennel that are too tough to use. Roughly chop the central fronds. Cut the fennel in half and then cut each half into 6 segments (or 4 if you're using smaller fennel) — each segment should have part of the core to help it stay intact. Cook the fennel in salted boiling water for 12–15 minutes until tender, then drain and leave to cool. Preheat your oven to 180°C (350°F/Gas 4).

Use baking paper to line a baking tray large enough to hold all the fennel. Lay out the fennel on the tray. Mix the oil and garlic together and pour over the fennel. Sprinkle with the parmesan and chopped fennel fronds. Bake in the oven for about 30 minutes or until golden.

(Serves 4)

insalata di arance
orange salad

This combination of sweet orange and olive oil is just beautiful. You can also add a handful of black olives and half a thinly sliced red onion.

3 oranges, cut into small cubes, with skin and pith removed
4 tablespoons extra virgin olive oil
½ teaspoon chilli flakes

Put the orange cubes in a bowl, drizzle with the olive oil and add the chilli flakes and some salt. Mix well and serve.
(Serves 4)

broccoli rabe

This is a lovely dish to go with porchetta or any other pork dish. It also works wonderfully well as a base for frittata (page 37). Broccoli rabe is now readily available in good fruit and vegie shops, but I often pick the wild variety which is much more bitter to eat — an acquired taste.

1 bunch broccoli rabe
4 tablespoons olive oil
1 garlic clove, chopped

Bring a large pot of salted water to the boil. Meanwhile, discard any outer leaves of rabe that are damaged or yellow and any tough stems. Chop the rest into 10 cm (4 inch) pieces. Boil for 5–10 minutes and then drain.

Heat the oil in a frying pan, add the garlic and cook over low heat for 30 seconds without browning. Add the rabe and cook, stirring, for about 10 minutes. Season with salt and pepper.
(Serves 4)

🌺 **fagioli con pomodoro**
green beans with tomato

3 tablespoons olive oil
1 garlic clove, finely chopped
400 g (14 oz) tin Italian chopped tomatoes
500 g (1 lb 2 oz) green beans (use any variety, but I prefer the flat ones), trimmed

Heat the oil in a saucepan that is large enough to later hold all the beans. Add the garlic and fry gently for about 1 minute. Add the tomatoes and cook for about 5 minutes. Add the beans, some salt and pepper and 125 ml (4 fl oz/½ cup) of water. Turn the heat to low and cook until the beans are tender. These beans are just as good served cold as they are hot.
(Serves 4)

cavolfiore con olive verde

braised cauliflower with green olives

1 small cauliflower
4 tablespoons olive oil
1 red onion, thinly sliced
100 g (3½ oz/½ cup) green olives

Cut the cauliflower into small florets and wash them. Heat the oil over medium heat in a large pan or frying pan with a lid. Add the onion and cauliflower, put the lid on the pan and simmer gently for 15–20 minutes, tossing the cauliflower occasionally. The lid will produce steam to keep the cauliflower moist, but check it isn't drying out and add a little water if necessary. Add the olives and cook for another 10 minutes, then take off the lid and brown a little before serving. (Serves 4)

insalata di finocchio

fennel salad

This is another very simple side salad that can easily be jazzed up with extras if you like. Try adding one orange, cut into cubes; half a roughly chopped iceberg lettuce; or the cubed orange plus some radicchio leaves.

1 fennel bulb with some fronds
2 tablespoons lemon juice
4 tablespoons olive oil

Remove the outer leaves of the fennel, cut in half, then cut the fennel into thin slices and put in a bowl. Mix the lemon juice and oil together with salt to taste. Pour over the fennel, mix through and sprinkle the fronds on top.
(Serves 4)

biete con pomodoro e aglio
silverbeet with tomato and garlic

1 bunch of silverbeet
3 tablespoons olive oil
2 garlic cloves, finely chopped
4 ripe tomatoes, diced or 400 g (14 oz) tin Italian chopped tomatoes
1 teaspoon chilli flakes (optional)

Bring a large pot of salted water to the boil. Chop the silverbeet into bite-sized pieces (I use the stalks and the leaves — as I've said, Sicilians never waste anything). Add the stalks to the water first and cook for 5 minutes or until tender, then add the leaves and cook for another 5 minutes. Drain, keeping about ½ cupful of the cooking water.

Heat the oil in the same pot and fry the garlic gently for about 1 minute. Add the tomatoes and cook for 5 minutes. Add the silverbeet, season and add the chilli, if using. Cover and cook for 10 minutes. If it looks in danger of drying out, add a little of the reserved cooking water. (Serves 4)

carciofi ripieni
stuffed artichokes

There are roughly three different types of artichokes available: purple and green with spikes; purple and green without spikes; and light green ones. I like to buy the slightly green and purple ones without the spikes. I find they don't have as much furry choke in the middle.

6 globe artichokes

2 lemons

160 g (5½ oz/2 cups) fresh
    white breadcrumbs

60 g (2 oz/½ cup) grated parmesan cheese

1 garlic clove, finely chopped

3 tablespoons chopped Italian
    (flat-leaf) parsley

125 ml (4 fl oz/½ cup) olive oil

3 eggs, lightly beaten

440 g (15½ oz) tin Italian
    tomatoes, puréed

With a serrated knife, slice off the top third of each artichoke (we want them to have flat tops). Cut off the bottom stalk as near to the leaves as possible so the artichoke has a flat bottom too. Don't discard the stalks: cut off the woody part and keep the tender part, usually about 2–3 cm (1 inch) from the bottom of the artichoke, and peel. As you prepare them, put your artichokes in a plastic bucket full of water into which you've squeezed the juice of the lemons (throw in the lemons as well, for good luck). The acid in the water will prevent the artichokes discolouring.

Preheat the oven to 190°C (375°F/Gas 5). Mix the breadcrumbs, parmesan, garlic and parsley together with some salt and pepper. Work with one artichoke at a time, leaving the rest in the water. Place the flat side of the artichoke down on a tea towel and push down on it with the palm of your hand. You want to open the leaves so give it a little push from side to side, not too hard. You still want it to keep its shape. Take some of the breadcrumb mixture and fill in between the leaves. You don't need to fill each section but just as much as you can. Don't worry about the very centre where the leaves are too tight to fill.

When you've stuffed all of the artichokes, heat the olive oil in a large non-stick frying pan. Take one artichoke at a time, dip the top in the beaten egg and then place, top down, in the pan. This is to seal the breadcrumbs inside the artichoke and should only take 1–2 minutes.

You will need a baking dish that will hold all the artichokes snugly and upright in a single layer. When all the artichokes are in the dish, sealed side up, pour in the tomatoes, 500 ml (17 fl oz/

2 cups) of water, a little salt and pepper and the artichoke stalks. Cover tightly with foil and bake for about 1½ hours. The timing will depend on the size of the artichokes but if a skewer glides through the centre really easily they should be cooked. It is better to overcook for this recipe rather than undercook: they need to be lovely and tender. Lift the corner of the foil occasionally: if the sauce starts to dry out during the cooking time, just add a little more water.

When eating artichokes, you don't eat the outer leaves but scrape the flesh from the inner leaves with your teeth. Towards the centre it gets tender and you can eat the whole thing.
(Serves 6)

finocchio selvatico
wild fennel

Where I live in Victoria, August to October is about the time to collect wild fennel. With the spring rains it starts to pop up along railway lines and country roads. It doesn't have a bulb and looks a little like dill but has a much stronger taste. Simply cut the plant at ground level with a sharp knife — it should be tender, but if it is at all stalky it's too far gone. Serve this as a side dish with lamb or pork. You can also use half the amount to make a base for a frittata (page 37). Or mix it with ricotta and a cupful of grated parmesan for a cannelloni filling.

1 good-sized bunch of wild fennel
4 tablespoons olive oil
1 garlic clove, finely chopped

Wash the fennel in salted water (the salt helps to kill any little bugs). Bring a large pot of water to the boil, chop the fennel roughly and add to the pot. Cook for 10–15 minutes until the stalks are tender and then drain.

Heat the oil in a large frying pan over medium heat. Add the garlic and cook for about 30 seconds, then add the fennel. Cook, stirring, for 10–15 minutes until tender. Season with salt and pepper before serving.
(Serves 4)

insalata di patate, pomodori e cetrioli

potato, tomato and cucumber salad

500 g (1 lb 2 oz) waxy salad potatoes
2 Lebanese cucumbers, sliced
3 tomatoes, cut into small wedges
1 small salad onion, thinly sliced
125 ml (4 fl oz/½ cup) extra virgin olive oil
1 tablespoon chopped dried oregano

Boil the potatoes in their skins until tender, then drain and set aside until cooled enough to handle. Peel off the skins and leave to cool.

Put the cucumbers, tomatoes and onion in a bowl. Chop the potatoes into bite-sized pieces and add to the bowl with the olive oil, oregano and salt to taste. Mix together well.
(Serves 5–6)

eggplant parmigiana

I also make this dish without the tomato sauce. Instead, as the eggplant comes out of the oven, I sprinkle it with a little red wine vinegar, torn basil leaves and chopped garlic.

3–4 eggplants (aubergines)
salt
250 ml (9 fl oz/1 cup) olive oil
½ quantity tomato pasta sauce (page 84)
50 g (1¾ oz/½ cup) grated parmesan cheese
basil leaves

Cut the eggplants vertically or horizontally into thin (1.5 cm/½ inch) slices. Layer the eggplant in a dish or colander, sprinkling each layer generously with salt, and leave for 1–2 hours. The salt will draw out the moisture and bitterness. Pat the eggplant dry with a tea towel (without rinsing).

Heat the oven to 220°C (425°F/Gas 7). Using a pastry brush, generously brush each slice of eggplant on both sides with the olive oil and place in a single layer on an oiled baking tray (if you don't have enough room or trays, cook the eggplant in batches). Bake on the lowest shelf of the oven for about 10 minutes, then turn them and cook for 5 minutes or until golden brown.

Arrange a layer of eggplant over a large serving plate, then spoon on some tomato sauce and spread evenly. Sprinkle with a little parmesan and some torn basil leaves. Repeat the layers until you've used up the ingredients. Delicious hot or cold.

Alternatively, put the eggplant in a baking dish. Repeat the method above, but when you've finished, mix a beaten egg with a cupful of tomato sauce, pour over the eggplant and bake at 180°C (350°F/Gas 4) for 40 minutes.

(Serves 6)

insalata di zucchine
marinated zucchini

6–8 small zucchini (courgettes)
1 tablespoon salt
2 garlic cloves, very finely chopped
125 ml (4 fl oz/½ cup) olive oil
4 tablespoons balsamic vinegar
3 tablespoons finely chopped mint

Slice the zucchini lengthways with a potato peeler, pressing hard to get a thicker slice. If you have a mandolin, use that for lovely clean slices.

Put the zucchini in a bowl, sprinkle with the salt and toss well. Leave for 1 hour for the salt to draw out the moisture. Drain the zucchini, squeezing to get rid of the liquid. Put in a serving bowl with the garlic, oil, vinegar and mint and mix well. Leave to stand at room temperature for about 30 minutes before serving.

(Serves 6)

insalata di cavolfiore
cauliflower salad

1 small cauliflower, cut into small florets
1 small red onion, thinly sliced
6 anchovy fillets, finely chopped
100 g (3½ oz/½ cup) chopped pitted black olives
2 tablespoons small salted capers, rinsed
3 roasted red capsicums (peppers), julienned
4 tablespoons olive oil
3 tablespoons red wine vinegar
2 tablespoons roughly chopped mint

Cook the cauliflower in boiling salted water for about 5 minutes until tender. Drain and set aside to cool.

Put the cauliflower in a bowl, add the onion, anchovies, olives, capers and capsicum and toss well. Mix the oil and vinegar together with the mint. Pour over the salad, toss and leave to sit for at least an hour before serving.

(Serves 4)

cotoletta di melanzane
crumbed eggplant

3 small eggplants (aubergines)
lots of salt
150 g (5 oz/1½ cups) dry breadcrumbs
75 g (2½ oz/¾ cup) grated parmesan or pecorino cheese
3 tablespoons chopped Italian (flat-leaf) parsley
1 garlic clove, finely chopped
3 eggs, lightly beaten
olive oil, for frying

Cut the eggplants vertically or horizontally into thin (1.5 cm/½ inch) slices. Layer the eggplant in a dish or colander, sprinkling each layer generously with salt, and leave for 1–2 hours. The salt will draw out the moisture and bitterness.

Put the breadcrumbs, cheese, parsley and garlic in a bowl, mix well and season. Put the beaten eggs in a different bowl.

Wipe the eggplant dry with a tea towel, without rinsing. Dip into the beaten eggs, then into the breadcrumbs, patting down to make sure it is thoroughly coated.

Heat some olive oil in a non-stick frying pan over medium heat and fry the eggplant slices for 5 minutes until golden (you'll need to do this in batches). Turn over and fry on the other side, then drain on kitchen paper. Serve hot or cold.

(Serves 6)

zucca con aglio e prezzemolo
mashed pumpkin with garlic and parsley

This is my version of mashed pumpkin. Use butternut, or any other variety of pumpkin you particularly like.

1 kg (2 lb 4 oz) pumpkin, peeled and cut into small pieces
2 garlic cloves, roughly chopped
4 Italian (flat-leaf) parsley sprigs, plus 1 tablespoon chopped parsley
125 ml (4 fl oz/½ cup) olive oil

Put the pumpkin in a large saucepan with a lid. Add the garlic, parsley and oil along with some salt and pepper, put the lid on and cook over very low heat, stirring occasionally. The lid will help the pumpkin produce some moisture in the pot, but if it starts to stick add a little water — no more than 3 tablespoons at a time.

When all the pumpkin has broken down, take off the lid and give it a good stir (it should have the same consistency as mashed potatoes). Check for salt and pepper and sprinkle with chopped parsley to serve.

(Serves 6)

caponata

3 eggplants (aubergines), diced
salt
5–6 celery stalks from the heart of the celery
6 long red capsicums (peppers)
250 ml (9 fl oz/1 cup) olive oil
1 large red onion, cut in half, then sliced
1 garlic clove, finely chopped
4 tablespoons small salted capers, rinsed
3 tablespoons red wine vinegar

Put the eggplant cubes in a colander over a bowl, lightly salt them and set aside for 1 hour for the salt to draw out the moisture and bitterness.

Cut the celery, including the leaves, into 1–2 cm (½ inch) pieces. Cut the capsicums in half lengthways and then slice widthways. I like to cook each vegetable separately as they all take different times, then mix them together at the end.

Tip the eggplant into a clean tea towel and pat dry. Heat 3 tablespoons of the olive oil in a frying pan over medium heat, then add the eggplant and cook for 10–15 minutes until tender and golden (don't overcrowd the pan, so cook in batches if necessary). You may need to add a little extra oil as the eggplant can soak up a lot of it. Drain on kitchen paper.

Heat another 3 tablespoons of oil in the pan, add the celery and onion and cook over medium–low heat until the celery is tender. Drain on kitchen paper.

Now add another 3 tablespoons of oil to the pan and cook the capsicums over medium heat until soft. Add the garlic and stir for a minute.

Mix all the vegetables in a large bowl, season with a little salt, add the capers and vinegar and mix well. Serve warm with a meat dish or as part of an antipasto plate.

(Serves 6)

Because mum had ten brothers and sisters and she was the eldest, there was little age difference between me and some of the younger aunties and uncles. In fact, I am 18 months older than mum's youngest brother. When we were growing up we were all great friends and would often go to dances together. This was wonderful for me because, as a young Italian girl, I was not allowed to go dancing without a chaperone, of course.

dolce

Sicilians are renowned throughout Italy for making the best cakes and biscuits, along with their famous gelati, of course. Pistachios, hazelnuts, walnuts and almonds are to be found in the wonderful biscuits. Ricotta is used for cakes and cannoli. Sicilians also adore marzipan and most sweet shops have marzipan fruits on display. At Easter little lambs are made out of marzipan and given to the children.

crostata di cioccolato e nocciole
chocolate and hazelnut tart

PASTRY
200 g (7 oz/1⅓ cups) plain
    (all-purpose) flour
140 g (5 oz) unsalted butter, chilled,
    cut into small cubes
½ teaspoon baking powder
4 tablespoons sugar
grated zest of ½ orange
1 egg, lightly beaten
2 tablespoons Marsala

FILLING
280 g (10 oz/2 cups) roasted hazelnuts
125 g (4½ oz) dark chocolate
90 g (3 oz) unsalted butter
150 g (5 oz/⅔ cup) sugar
grated zest of ½ orange
2 eggs, lightly beaten
1 tablespoon plain (all-purpose) flour
3 tablespoons Marsala

In an electric mixer with a paddle attachment, beat the flour, butter, baking powder, sugar and orange zest for about 3 minutes. Add the egg and Marsala and beat until it just comes together. Tip out onto a floured work surface and gently knead until smooth. Roll the dough out quickly (as the dough softens it becomes harder to work with). Grease a deep 25 cm (10 inch) tart tin and line with the dough, pricking the base all over with a fork. Chill for 30 minutes. Preheat the oven to 200°C (400°F/Gas 6).

To make the filling, grind the hazelnuts in the food processor until they look like coarse breadcrumbs. Transfer to a bowl, then chop the chocolate in the processor to the same consistency and add to the bowl.

Beat the butter, sugar and orange zest until light and creamy. Add the eggs and flour and beat for a further couple of minutes. Add this to the hazelnut and chocolate mixture and mix gently with a wooden spoon. Spoon into the chilled pastry base and bake for 30 minutes, or until the filling feels firm in the centre. Cool a little before serving.

(Serves 8–10)

🌺 torta di ricotta
ricotta cake

If I'm buying ricotta I like to choose from the large moulds — I find the smaller ones too soft and moist. If you can only find the softer ricotta, just drain it overnight in a colander sitting over a bowl.

PASTRY
1 quantity chocolate and hazelnut tart pastry dough (previous page)

FILLING
115 g (4 oz/½ cup) chopped dried figs
3 tablespoons Marsala
750 g (1 lb 10 oz) fresh firm ricotta
115 g (4 oz/½ cup) sugar
1 egg, lightly beaten, plus 1 egg white, for glazing
2 tablespoons honey
90 g (3 oz/⅔ cup) roasted hazelnuts
grated zest of ½ orange

Make the pastry as for the previous recipe and use it to line a 22 cm (8½ inch) tart tin. Keep the pastry trimmings. Chill for 30 minutes. Preheat the oven to 200°C (400°F/Gas 6), line the pastry case with baking paper and baking beads or uncooked rice and blind bake for 15 minutes. Remove the paper and beads and leave the pastry case to cool. Turn down the oven to 190°C (375°F/Gas 5).

Meanwhile, to make the filling, soak the chopped figs in the Marsala for about 30 minutes. Whisk the ricotta with the sugar, egg and honey until creamy, then add the figs and Marsala, hazelnuts and orange zest. Gently mix it all together.

Pour the filling evenly into the pastry case. Roll out any pastry trimmings, cut into strips and arrange in a lattice pattern on top of the filling. Brush the pastry with the egg white. Bake for 35–40 minutes or until the top turns golden. Serve at room temperature.
(Serves 8–10)

biscotti di fichi e anice

fig and aniseed biscuits

This is a recipe my daughter Francesca has made for years. The biscuits keep well and are something lovely to have in the cupboard for visitors. Instead of the figs and aniseeds you could use your own combinations: try chocolate and almonds; date and walnuts; or pistachios and glazed orange. The quantities don't really matter as long as the basic ingredients are there.

300 g (10 oz/2 cups) plain (all-purpose) flour
225 g (8 oz/1 cup) sugar
1 teaspoon baking powder
½ teaspoon salt
1 large egg yolk
3 tablespoons milk
125 ml (4 fl oz/½ cup) olive oil
½ teaspoon vanilla extract
375 g (13 oz/2 cups) chopped dried figs
2 teaspoons aniseeds

Preheat the oven to 190°C (375°F/Gas 5). Mix the flour, sugar, baking powder and salt with electric beaters for a few minutes. Beat the egg yolk into the milk and then add the oil and vanilla. Pour into the flour mixture and beat gently, just for a few minutes, until smooth, adding more milk if needed. Only beat until the mixture just comes together.

Add the figs and aniseeds and knead gently. Divide the mixture in half and roll each portion into a log about 30 cm (12 inches) long and 5 cm (2 inches) wide.

Line a baking tray with greased baking paper (you might need to line 2 trays). Put the logs on the tray and bake for 30 minutes or until firm. Remove from the oven and cool slightly, then cut into 1.5 cm (½ inch) slices on the diagonal. Turn the oven down to 160°C (315°F/Gas 2–3).

Put the slices back on the baking tray and put them back in the oven. Bake for 5–10 minutes until slightly golden. Cool on wire racks.

(Makes about 48)

biscotti di mandorla e pinoli
almond and pine nut biscuits

250 g (9 oz) blanched almonds
3 heaped tablespoons pine nuts
75 g (2½ oz/½ cup) plain (all-purpose) flour
75 g (2½ oz/⅓ cup) caster (superfine) sugar
15 g (½ oz) unsalted butter, at room temperature
grated zest of ½ lemon
1 egg, lightly beaten
1 tablespoon grappa

Preheat the oven to 140°C (275°F/Gas 1). Roughly chop the almonds and 2 tablespoons of the pine nuts in a food processor until about the same size as large grains of rice. Tip into a bowl and add the flour, sugar, butter, lemon zest, egg and grappa. Use your hands to mix and knead it all together. Line a baking tray with baking paper and grease with butter.

Moisten your hands with a little water and roll about 1 heaped teaspoon of the mixture into a ball (the dough will be quite chunky). Place on the baking tray and flatten slightly with the palm of your hand. Carry on until you've rolled out all the dough — you will need to wash your hands a few times and keep them moistened because the dough will be sticky. Place a whole pine nut on top of each biscuit and bake on the top shelf of the oven for about 20 minutes.

Turn the heat up to 150°C (300°F/Gas 2) and cook for 10 minutes. Cool on a wire rack. (Makes about 40)

buccellato
fruit crescent

There are many different versions of this recipe and you may choose to leave something out or add your own ideas. It is lovely to serve at Christmas.

PASTRY
400 g (14 oz) plain (all-purpose) flour
150 g (5 oz) icing (confectioner's) sugar
175 g (6 oz) unsalted butter, cut into
  cubes and softened
3 egg yolks
grated zest of 1 orange
1 egg, beaten, for glazing

FILLING
125 g (4 oz) dried figs, finely chopped
50 g (1¾ oz) raisins, finely chopped
100 g (3½ oz) dates, finely chopped
150 ml (5 fl oz) Marsala
1 teaspoon ground cinnamon
grated zest and juice of 1 orange
200 g (7 oz) honey
150 g (5 oz) hazelnuts, chopped

To make the filling, put the chopped fruit in a bowl with the Marsala, cinnamon, orange zest and juice and leave to macerate overnight.

Put the soaked fruit in a saucepan with the honey and cook over low heat until sticky and firm. Take off the heat, add the hazelnuts and leave to cool.

To make the pastry, gently blend the flour, sugar, butter, egg yolks, orange zest and a pinch of salt in a food processor until the dough just comes together. You may need to add a few tablespoons of cold water to bring it together. Take out and knead gently until you have a soft ball. Place plastic wrap down on a work surface, put the pastry on the plastic and roll out to a rough rectangle about 45 x 15 cm (about 18 x 6 inches). This is a rough measurement; you just need to have a roll. Cover with plastic and lift the pastry gently, place on a baking tray and chill for 1 hour.

Spoon the filling down one side of the pastry, then gently fold the pastry over the filling. Moisten the edge with the beaten egg and press down firmly. Trim any uneven edges — you should now have a log shape. Cut about 4 slits at intervals in the top of the pastry then gently turn in the ends of the log to form a crescent. Put on a line baking tray, brush with the remaining egg and chill for 30 minutes. Preheat the oven to 160°C (315°F/Gas 2–3). Bake for 30–35 minutes or until golden. Dust with icing sugar.

(Serves 8–10)

cannoli

This amount of ricotta filling is enough for all 25 cannoli. Once you've fried the cannoli shells, they keep very well in an airtight container for up to 3 months (I lay kitchen paper between the layers when I store them). But they don't keep well once they're filled. So you could do as I do and make 25 cannoli, store half and fill 12 — in which case, reduce the filling quantity by half. To make cannoli you will need a pasta machine and metal cannoli tubes (from speciality kitchenware shops).

CANNOLI
320 g (11 oz) plain (all-purpose) flour
1 tablespoon dark cocoa powder
2 tablespoons caster (superfine) sugar
50 g (1¾ oz) cold unsalted butter, diced
170 ml (5½ fl oz/⅔ cup) Marsala
2 litres (8 cups) vegetable oil, for frying
1 egg white, for sealing

FILLING
1 kg (2 lb 4 oz) fresh firm ricotta
175 g (6 oz/½ cup) honey
3 tablespoons sugar
125 ml (4 fl oz/½ cup) Marsala
grated zest of ½ lemon
icing (confectioner's) sugar, for dusting

To make the cannoli, mix the flour, cocoa, sugar and butter with an electric mixer with a dough attachment until the butter mixes right down. Slowly add the Marsala until the dough comes together (it should be quite firm, as if for making pasta). Wrap in plastic and leave for 1 hour.

I find using a pasta machine much quicker and easier than rolling the cannoli by hand. Cut the dough into 4 portions. Flatten the dough with the palm of your hand until as flat as possible. Now roll the dough several times through the widest setting of your pasta machine until it starts to become smooth. Turn the machine down a notch and roll again. Now turn it to setting number 3 and cut the sheets of dough in half so they are easier to handle. Roll the dough again and then lay out flat and cut into approximately 8 cm (3 inch) circles with a cutter. You can re-roll the remaining scraps of dough, but only the once; after that it must be discarded.

In a saucepan large enough to hold about 5 cannoli shells at a time, heat the oil to 190°C (375°F) or until a scrap of pastry dropped into the oil bubbles. Wrap a circle of dough around the tube and seal the join with egg white. Drop into the oil and cook for 2–3 minutes until the pastry blisters up on the outside. Take them out of the oil and drain on kitchen paper. When cool enough to handle, slide the cannoli off the metal tube.

To fill the cannoli, beat the ricotta, honey, sugar, Marsala and lemon zest until creamy. Spoon into a piping bag to pipe into the cannoli. Only fill when you're ready to eat or they will go soft. Dust with lots of icing sugar.

(Makes 25)

# ravioli dolci
sweet fried ravioli

PASTRY
½ quantity cannoli pastry without the cocoa (page 216)

FILLING
100 g (3½ oz/½ cup) sultanas
3 tablespoons Marsala
300 g (10 oz) fresh firm ricotta
175 g (6 oz/½ cup) honey
1 tablespoon sugar
1 teaspoon ground cinnamon
vegetable oil, for frying
icing (confectioner's) sugar, for dusting

Roll out the cannoli pastry with a pasta machine, as on page 216, and cut into 10 cm (4 inch) diameter circles. Meanwhile, soak the sultanas in the Marsala for about 30 minutes. Beat the ricotta, honey, sugar and cinnamon until creamy. Stir in the sultanas and Marsala.

Spoon a tablespoon of the ricotta filling into the centre of each pastry circle, then fold over and join the edges together, pressing firmly with a fork. There should be no gaps (if there are any gaps you'll lose all the filling while they cook).

Pour enough vegetable oil into a small saucepan to come up 6–7 cm (2½ inches) from the top of the pan. Heat to about 190°C (375°F) or until a scrap of pastry dropped into the oil bubbles. Add a few ravioli at a time to the oil. When they start to turn golden brown, lift them out and drain on kitchen paper. Dust with icing sugar and serve warm.
(Makes 12–14)

torta di mandorla, cioccolato e marsala

almond, chocolate and marsala cake

300 g (10 oz) blanched almonds
200 g (7 oz) dark chocolate, chopped into small pieces
100 g (3½ oz) dark cocoa powder
250 g (9 oz) unsalted butter
250 g (9 oz) caster (superfine) sugar
5 eggs, lightly beaten
3 tablespoons dry Marsala
icing (confectioner's) sugar, for dusting

Line a 24 cm (9½ inch) cake tin with baking paper and grease well. Preheat the oven to 160°C (315°F/Gas 2–3). Finely chop the almonds and chocolate in a food processor, then add the cocoa and process for 2 minutes. Tip out into a bowl.

Mix the butter and sugar in the food processor until light and creamy. Add the eggs one at a time, mixing well after each one. Pour into the bowl with the chocolate almonds and add the Marsala. Mix well.

Spoon into the tin, smooth the surface and bake for 45 minutes. Serve with ricotta or cream. (Serves 12)

nuvoletti
little clouds

3 eggs
250 g (9 oz) caster (superfine) sugar
300 g (10 oz/2 cups) plain (all-purpose) flour

Preheat the oven to 170°C (325°F/Gas 3) and line a baking tray with baking paper. Beat the eggs and sugar until stiff peaks form. Sift the flour three times into another bowl. Add 3 tablespoons of sifted flour to the eggs and mix gently, then continue adding 3 tablespoons of flour at a time, stirring gently. Place teaspoons of mixture on the tray and bake for 10 minutes.
(Makes about 50)

torrone
almond toffee

500 g (1 lb 2 oz) almonds
1 tablespoon vegetable oil
400 g (14 oz) caster (superfine) sugar

Preheat the oven to 200°C (400°F/Gas 6). Arrange the almonds on a baking tray and roast in the oven for 6–7 minutes. Remove the almonds from the tray and leave to cool. Brush the baking tray with the oil and set aside.

Put the almonds, sugar and 3 tablespoons of water in a large saucepan and stir over low heat until the sugar dissolves. Then cook, shaking the pan occasionally, until the sugar caramelises and turns light brown. Take off the heat and quickly pour into the baking tray. Working quickly, use an oiled spatula to flatten the toffee. Set aside until cool enough to handle. Cut into squares (don't worry if they are a little rough) and leave until cooled completely. This will keep well in an airtight container (my mother always has this in her cupboard).
(Makes many pieces, depending on what size you cut them)

🌸 mazarisi

pistachio cakes

200 g (7 oz) shelled pistachio nuts
4 eggs, separated, plus 2 egg yolks
150 g (5 oz) caster (superfine) sugar
50 g (1¾ oz) potato flour
grated zest of 1 orange
icing (confectioner's) sugar, for dusting

Heat the oven to 160°C (315°F/Gas 2–3). Butter two 12-hole muffin tins. Blanch the pistachios in boiling water for 1 minute, then drain and place them in a tea towel. Rub them with the towel to remove as much skin as possible. Grind them finely in a food processor and set aside.

Beat the 4 egg whites with a pinch of salt until soft peaks form. In a separate bowl, mix the 6 egg yolks with the sugar for about 4 minutes until thick and pale. Stir in the potato flour, orange zest and ground pistachios, then gently fold in the egg whites. Spoon the mixture into the muffin tins so they are about two-thirds full. Bake in the oven for 30 minutes. Leave to cool in the tins for 5–10 minutes, then turn out onto a rack to cool. Dust with icing sugar and serve with a cup of coffee.

(Makes about 24)

palle di ricotta
ricotta balls

450 g (1 lb) fresh firm ricotta
4 eggs, lightly beaten
85 g (3 oz) plain (all-purpose) flour
50 g (1¾ oz) unsalted butter, softened
grated zest of ½ orange
vegetable oil, for frying
200 g (7 oz) very good honey, for drizzling

Beat the ricotta in an electric mixer until creamy, then add the eggs and beat well. Turn the mixer to low and add the flour, a little at a time. Add the butter, orange zest and a pinch of salt. Beat well and set aside until ready to use.

Pour in enough oil to half-fill a saucepan and place over medium heat. Drop a small piece of batter into the oil to test the temperature: when the batter floats, the oil is hot enough to cook.

Take a spoonful of batter, about the size of a golf ball, and use another spoon to push it into the oil. Don't overcrowd the pan by cooking too many at once. When the ricotta balls are golden on one side, turn them over. I like to move them around a little with the spoon as they are cooking. They don't need to cook too fast and they won't puff up if the oil is too hot. When cooked, lift them out with a slotted spoon and drain on kitchen paper for a few minutes. Put in a serving bowl and drizzle with honey while still hot (as much as you like). Serve immediately. (Serves 6–8)

peparelli
honey and almond biscotti

These biscuits have been in our family for a very long time. As far back as I can remember they have always been in the cupboard, at my house, my mother's and all my aunts'.

1 kg (2 lb 4 oz) plain (all-purpose) flour
300 g (10 oz) caster (superfine) sugar
1 heaped teaspoon bicarbonate of soda
1 teaspoon ground cinnamon
250 ml (9 fl oz/1 cup) olive oil
3 eggs, lightly beaten
300 g (10 oz) honey
grated zest and juice of 1 orange
250 ml (9 fl oz/1 cup) Marsala
300 g (10 oz/2 cups) chopped almonds

Preheat the oven to 190°C (375°F/Gas 5). Mix the flour, sugar, bicarbonate of soda and cinnamon in a bowl and make a well in the centre. Mix together the oil, eggs, honey, orange zest and juice and Marsala and tip into the well. Add the almonds. Stir with a wooden spoon until well mixed. Knead lightly and divide into 4 portions. Roll each portion into a log.

Line a large baking tray with baking paper (you might need to line 2 trays to hold 2 logs each). Put the logs on the trays and bake for 25 minutes or until light brown and firm. Remove from the oven and leave to cool slightly, then cut into 1.5 cm (½ inch) slices on the diagonal.

There are two ways to finish off these biscuits: my aunts each have a different method. If you like a softer texture don't rebake the biscuits. If you like a harder, crunchier biscuit, put the slices back onto the baking tray in a single layer and put them back into the oven you have turned off. Leave them in there until cool. Maybe the first time you make these you could try half and half and see which you prefer.

(Makes about 48)

In Catania we were lucky enough to live in a large farmhouse on the outskirts of the city. Liquorice used to grow on the farm and I vividly remember going out to the field, picking some straight from the ground and eating it. I have such wonderful memories of this house that when I finally went back to Sicily I couldn't wait to go and see it. I found it had been replaced by a freeway and a block of apartments...

🌺 index

 # thank you

There have been so many people, friends and family, who have assisted me on the journey that has led to this book. Too many to mention you all by name; but some I must. Firstly, my mother, who passed on some of the recipes and techniques and also demonstrated that cooking is never a chore born out of necessity, rather it's full of passion, love and fun. My husband, Colin, who is not only my worst critic but also my most supportive fan. My daughter, Francesca, and son, Clark, for similar reasons, but at least they have computer skills. Brigitte Hafner for giving me confidence in my own ability. To Richard Cornish, Jane Lawson, Paul Stokes and Tim White for their help and advice along the way.

Published in 2009 by Murdoch Books Pty Limited

Murdoch Books Australia
Pier 8/9, 23 Hickson Road
Millers Point NSW 2000
Phone: +61 (0) 2 8220 2000
Fax: +61 (0) 2 8220 2558
www.murdochbooks.com.au

Murdoch Books UK Limited
Erico House, 6th Floor
93–99 Upper Richmond Road
Putney, London SW15 2TG
Phone: +44 (0) 20 8785 5995
Fax: +44 (0) 20 8785 5985
www.murdochbooks.co.uk

Chief Executive: Juliet Rogers
Publishing Director: Kay Scarlett
Publisher: Jane Lawson
Design Concept and Layout: Hugh Ford
Illustrations: Hugh Ford
Photography: Alan Benson
Rosa's Assistant: Jess McIntosh
Styling: Sarah O'Brien
Production: Alexandra Gonzalez

National Library of Australia
Cataloguing-in-Publication Data:
Mitchell, Rosa. My Cousin Rosa/Rosa
Mitchell. Includes index.
ISBN 978 1 741963 632 (hbk.) Cookery,
Italian–Sicilian style. 641.59458

Printed by 1010 Printing International
Limited in 2009
PRINTED IN CHINA.